Mixed Emotions

By Sheyla Bonnick & Kit Garratt-Proctor

About the Author

Sheyla Bonnick

Sheyla Bonnick, a talented multi-instrumentalist, discovered her musical abilities instinctively, learning violin and piano in high school. After responding to an ad for dancers in Hannover, Germany, she was discovered singing and playing piano by a close friend of Donna Summer. Sheyla later joined the iconic group Boney M but left after a few months, recording singles for Hansa Records, including a disco version of "Proud Mary."

Sheyla married Icelandic bassist and producer Ingvar Areliusson, and they produced several acts together. Sheyla later reunited with Maizie Williams for a successful 9-year Boney M tour and now leads her own version of the group. Sheyla is also a singer, songwriter, author, designer, and artist, and recently released a viral Russian single. She remains a prolific voice on the UK soul scene.

Kit Garratt-Proctor

Kit Garratt-Proctor writes across many genres of fiction, including novels, plays and poetry. Kit has worked extensively in education, specialising in English Literature, Drama and Creative Writing. Kit combines his writing with character performance and presentation work.

Table of Contents

Chapter One – The Audition..1

   London 1974 1

   Paris 1967 11

   London 1974 15

Chapter Two – City of Dreams?...29

Chapter Three – Champagne for Everyone!.........................54

Chapter Four – The Ball Starts to Roll…?..........................79

Chapter Five – Some Enchanted Evening. 97

Chapter Six – 'Mr Dead.' 133

Chapter Seven – Be Careful What You Wish For….........157

Chapter Eight – Very Mixed Emotions...............................196

Chapter Nine – Lights! Camera! Chart Action…?............223

Chapter Ten – And we are all but playthings of the Gods.243

Epilogue 274

   England – One Year Later 274

Chapter One – The Audition

London 1974

The Roman centurion turned on his heels, causing the large sword that dangled from his waistband to swing within an inch of Satine's face. The situation was prevented from being particularly remarkable or terrifying as both Satine and the owner of the weapon were only two of thirty people crammed into the dingy, damp, and fetid dressing room.

In any event, the pretty Roman was far more concerned with his eyeliner than putting anyone to death, and he jostled with two other equally pretty young men in togas to get a prime position at one of the few mirrors in the narrow room. Although used to crowded chorus lines, this particular gig had been beyond the pale; the whole chorus was used to end both of the acts of this musical. The dressing room was barely comfortable for a dozen dancers at a time. At least getting into elaborate costumes was not an issue for all but the lucky handful playing Roman guards. For two key scenes, costumes of any kind were not a problem at all for this particular show as far as Satine and the rest of the 'citizens' or 'slaves' were concerned. As Satine glanced down briefly at her own cold but impressively youthful form, she realised that she didn't even notice her own nakedness anymore. Despite her initial reluctance to accept the job, there was nothing like six evening performances and two matinees a week to get you accustomed to baring all.

The musical was a celebration of the supposed life of Roman Emperor Nero, of the alleged penchant for fiddling while Rome burned around him. At least, he did in this particular show. The historical accuracy of the piece was clearly not something that troubled the writers or the producers, Satine had realised very early on in the run – (nobody but Satine had seemed to think it odd that Nero played a modern violin and, at one point, an electric guitar). The nakedness was part of a crowded dance routine that attempted to replicate a Roman orgy, as flames licked across the skyline of the great city. If the audience looked closely, the 'flames' were obviously bunches of crepe paper hoisted up on wires. Not that the audience was too distracted by the shortcomings of the set design when there were acres of dimly lit but nevertheless naked flesh on show. The pillars that collapsed onto the Bacchanalian chorus and their notorious Emperor were polystyrene and the world of Nero ended with a squeak rather than a bang or whimper. But that was showbusiness and the scandalous reputation of the show ensured packed houses. The critics, of course, had gone into a feeding frenzy and slated every aspect of the show including the main cast. For once, Satine had been grateful that her role was anonymous amidst the chorus line.

It had not even been Satine's idea to apply for the chorus. Ava had spotted the audition advert and insisted that they tried out. Satine heard of the play coming to England and the immediate fanfare of notoriety that had even made it to the House of Lords. It was the hot ticket, the copious amounts of naked Roman slaves cavorting on stage and stalking through the audience ensuring that the theatre had sold out for the entirety of the run - even before the previews had started! The audience members kidded themselves that they came for the string of songs that had already been turned into hit singles and the sense of 'culture' because it was set in the ancient world and therefore 'highbrow.' Satine knew that the majority of them came for the flashes of breasts and genitals that were unsuccessfully covered by long, itchy wigs that brought the female dancers out in painful rashes. The inclusion of the wigs for the female cast was the result of a court injunction. Apparently, penises would not taint the moral fibre of the British public if flaccid throughout their performance. Breasts too were fine and would cause no lasting harm to the moral majority. But vaginas? No. Vaginas were definitely against Queen and Country. Satine found this ridiculous and, as Ava had said rather loudly in the bar the night before- 'where would anyone be without vaginas? Why pretend they don't exist? The Queen has a vagina, doesn't she?' The last question had silenced the room like the arrival of a gunslinger in a Western. There were things you just did not say out loud, it seemed. Chief amongst them was any speculation concerning Royal genitalia. The irony of the fact that the people giving them both icy glares for the rest of their short stay in the bar had been sitting in the stalls half an hour earlier (gladly watching as much flesh as they could) was not wasted on either Satine or Ava. They had roared laughing all the way back to their shared bedsit.

As Satine pulled on the horrible nylon wig for (mercifully) the last time that weekend, she glanced across the room to where Ava was hastily adjusting her own mangled pile of yellow strands that had, for the first three days, resembled a Mary Hopkin mane. Satine had not been assigned the long, straight, and more flattering pieces that had been given out to the white girls. It would have been nice to have had some choice, Satine thought. Then again, at least there were four black members of the chorus in total which was,

4

percentagewise, a lot higher than the last three shows in which she had been involved. Needless to say, the main cast was all white – even though the female lead in the original Broadway production had been black. Apparently, the white girl cast in her place for the London run was, according to the director, 'the only choice for the part' of an Amazonian Queen forced into marriage with a Roman senator and lusted after by a jealous Nero. The fact that said actress had just left a dreary but astoundingly popular soap opera didn't exactly impede her case. Nor did the fact that she was sleeping with the impresario who had bankrolled the venture in the first place. The meaning of 'Amazonian' was clearly flexible if the figures aligned.

'Let's get it over with!' She yelled across the room to Ava, as the chorus began to move out. Over the loudspeakers in the dressing room, barely adequate warbling of a lament from the palest Amazonian in creation faded to limp applause. Moments later, the sound of the orchestra beginning the finale music filled the air. Ava waved and flashed Satine her beautiful, toothy grin. Within seconds, the dressing room was empty and the near naked Roman chorus was in full swing.

The light rain was refreshing that night as the two women strolled back to their digs. Passing a Radio Rentals shop, a host of televisions of all shapes and sizes flashing out that Saturday night's 'entertainment'. Satine felt the silent rage she always experienced when she saw the grotesque form of Minstrels singing and dancing on the mosaic of screens. Reading her thoughts, Ava scowled at the display and shouted:

'And they think that is the epitome of family entertainment!'

Satine shrugged, too tired to join in but somewhat calmed by the fact that Ava had been heard by a small group of teenagers who were standing by the shop front and hflashedad been watching the displays. In response, the group dropped their eyes and shuffled away.

The bedsit, the attic room of a dilapidated four-storey house, was only intended for one inhabitant at a time. The only access was via a narrow and steep stairway from the third floor. Neither of them smoked, and they prayed that the residents on the floors below either refrained from the habit themselves or at least didn't light up in bed. The house, and their room in particular, would have been a death trap. Still, it was cheap didn't eat into their shared wages, and was only 'home' for the duration of their run in the musical. Both were pleased that there were only three weeks left in some ways, but the uncertainty of where the next job would come from had already started to wake them up in the early hours.

A lumpy and narrow bed pulled out from the wall. However, four bruised knees and several cracked nails later, Satine and Ava had managed to put up an additional camp bed. A small kitchenette area with two gas rings, a sink, and a kettle took up nearly all the remaining space. They had painted the walls white and bedecked them with posters where the mould started to break through in black speckles. Clint Eastwood sneered down from one wall, Che Guevara from another, and, somewhat unexpectedly, Einstein poked his tongue out from above the kitchenette area.

The kettle had barely started to whistle when the door of the bedsit began to shake as an impatient knocking began. Opening the door, Ava was faced with the pinched, scowling carapace of their landlady, Mrs Shorvosky. Occupying the first two floors, Mrs Shorvosky was a dour little figure who seemed to be dressed permanently in a wrap-around pinny. Nobody seemed to know what had become of Mr Shorvosky and the only clue to there having ever been one was a small, yellowing photograph of a man in military attire who smiled out at new arrivals to the house from the wall opposite the front door. If the figure was a picture was of a young Mr Shorvosky, Satine had wondered if the smile was there because it had been taken before he had met his blushing bride! Her grey hair was long but scraped back into a bun and pinned into place so that it resembled something in a taxidermist's shop window. Her false teeth were far too large for her mean little beak of a mouth, and they gave an unpleasant sucking noise as she spoke:

'What have I told you about the telephone?!'

This was the nearest Ava and Satine were going to get to a greeting. Bracing herself for the familiar tirade, Ava attempted to smile as Mrs Shorvosky continued.

'I told you girls – as I tell ALL my guests – the telephone is mine and mine alone. I do not run an answering service for you, and I do not expect you to give my number out as if it were your own!'

'We don't give it out, Mrs Sh-' Satine began, rising from the camp bed to stand behind Ava in an automatic show of solidarity against the harridan. However, Mrs Shorvosky had clearly been stewing on this matter all day and was not to be stopped until she completed her rant.

'Furthermore, I do not expect to be asked to take down messages as if I were a common secretary! I told you clearly enough when you moved in – there is a perfectly good public telephone at the corner of the road.'

What Mrs Shorvosky didn't seem to realise was that the phone booth in question was the de facto office of a local pimp, a drug dealer and the favoured urinal of every drunk that staggered from the nearby pub after closing time.

'But we didn't give out your number,' Satine began again as she detected a pause in Mrs Shorvosky's diatribe. But this time it was Ava who interrupted Satine:

'Actually, Mrs Shorvosky, I did give the number out last week. But it was only because it was for work. It won't happen again. I am so sorry.' Ava flashed her dazzling grin and Satine found herself joining in without realising. The two stood stock still, their grins becoming a rictus and their jaws beginning to ache as the old woman stared at them for what seemed an eternity. At length, it seemed Mrs Shorvosky was satisfied that she had made her point.

'Yes… well, see that it doesn't happen again. Here!' She produced a piece of torn paper from under the folds of her pinny and handed it to Ava. Without a further word, she turned and headed back down the stairs. Satine waited until she could no longer hear the landlady's footsteps before speaking.

'So, who did you give her number to? Not that guy in the bar last week? He was a complete loser, Ava!'

'No,' Ava spun round to face Satine. Grinning again, but this time with genuine pleasure, she pressed the note into Satine's hand and said:

'The time of losers has gone, my friend! That note is our future!'

Satine looked down at the folded note and saw that their landlady had written down a London address, a date and a time. Although she could not have known it then, in the years to come, she would remember the moment Ava presented the note to her and the unlikely messenger who had reluctantly delivered it like a wraith from the Underworld. There were many times she would ponder that, had Mrs Shorvosky just binned the note in temper, what would their lives have gone on to be? Quieter, certainly. Happier? That remained to be seen.

Nevertheless, there would always be an ache in Satine's heart as she remembered the two young women they had been at the start of their adventure. Their innocence intact, their hopes so high for the potential of living a dream that they perhaps should have feared.

It would certainly come at a cost.

Paris 1967

The woman thought that she had died. Only for a few seconds, but nevertheless, her mind had filled with a peaceful acceptance that she had stepped away from life. The constriction around her throat had stopped burning; the frantic battle to breathe had dwindled away to nothing. For a time, she hovered in a space between consciousness and oblivion, seeming to look down upon herself as she lay on the destroyed bed. Then, exploding upwards from her chest, the gasp burst out of her mouth. In an instant she was lurching forwards, her hands finding the floor as she wretched out agonised breaths. Sucking in the hot, dry air of the room, the woman felt her lungs heave and expand and, slowly, her eyes began to focus.

As if moving under water, her hands drifted to her throat, as if she expected to find his iron fists clutching at her even now. Still disorientated, the woman began to jerk her head around the room with robotic stiffness. He was nowhere to be seen. She drew her feet up towards her chest, clutching her knees as her breathing turned to sobs. She gave in to the overwhelming wave of relief that rippled through her whole body, her breathing starting to calm as the sobs slowed and faded.

She sat completely still for a few moments, almost as if her entire body had gone into a trance. Then, she was on her feet, desperately pulling on the ripped and bloodied sweater that was hanging over the side of the bed. She found her jeans, pulling them up and ignoring the droplets of blood that fell onto them from the open cut on her forehead. She stood in the centre of the room, her eyes darting around as she took in the devastation. The dingy room was sparsely furnished, but what few items of furniture there were had been decimated. A small dressing table was covered with the shattered remains of the mirror that had hung on the wall above it. The little stool that belonged under the table was in pieces in a far corner of the room. The blind hung like a dead bird from only one chord, shaking in the icy breeze from the open window. She became aware of the sounds of the city, car horns angrily sounding in an unending chorus whilst shouts and laughter rang out from the busy bar directly below the room.

Then she saw him. Lying flat on his back, his arms spread out like an obscene parody of a crucifixion statue and his eyes staring blankly up at her. For a moment, it seemed as though he might stir again, and she instinctively backed against the wall. Then her eyes came to rest on the hilt of the knife, standing up in the centre of his chest. The blade was completely submerged in flesh, blood that was almost black welling around the handle. His knife. The one with which he had threatened to kill her only moments before.

The woman found that she could recall nothing of the final moments of their struggle. He had been on her, choking her until she had felt herself slipping away, her strength gone. Somehow, she had found a reserve of energy she did not know she had possessed. Her eyes fell to her hands, and she stared with appalled fascination at the blood on them that she knew was not her own.

Outside, an urban fox shrieked its high-pitched and jarring call.

Almost screaming out in shock at the shrill animal squeal, the woman clambered over the bed and got to her feet. The fox had been a shrill but effective alarm. She sprang into hectic action, locating her bag and gathering her few scattered belongings. Within three minutes, she was on the busy street, racing towards the all night gas station on the corner of the main road. Within fifteen minutes, she had returned to the flat, the cover of darkness mercifully hiding her ravaged appearance from the young attendant who took the money at the serving booth.

The woman poured the contents of the container she had promised to return to the young attendant once she had 'refilled her car' on every surface in the room, including the bed. She paused only a moment before doing the same to the figure of the man on the floor. The icy calm that had descended on the woman would not last, she knew. But the primal instinct to survive was driving her and she barely paused in her action until the can was empty. The mood of the city was different now: Paris was asleep, the only sounds were those of the dumpster trucks as the nocturnal street cleaning came to an end ahead of the dawn. In the distance, she could hear a baker's van being unloaded.

The woman had to wait for two of these dumpsters to drive by before she could risk walking away, fighting the urge to run. She flinched as she saw the flames licking up the exterior of the building from the open window of the room,

14

black smoke snaking into the purple sky as dawn started over the city. However, by the time the gas pipe ruptured and sent a fireball through the building -obliterating both it and the body inside, the woman was long gone.

London 1974

The office of Rosie and Reiman Shultz-Klopper made an encouraging impression. Not overly furnished, but the pieces were tasteful and clearly expensive. A modern, designer eye had selected the furnishing and lighting and both Satine and Ava felt reassured by the overall effect. Compared to other agents' offices, it had a feeling of quality about it and the smell of freshly brewing coffee added that continental appeal that London had not yet got to grips with to any real extent.

Satine had chosen a beautiful ensemble, very Spanish in overall look although she had sourced the entire outfit from Camden Market. The white silk of her blouse contrasted strikingly with the black bolero jacket she had matched with low heeled boots. Her jewellery was subtle but effective – the pearl earrings had been her grandmother's and the tiny diamond clip on her lapel had been a rare indulgence that Satine had allowed herself after getting the latest gig. Ava, by comparison, was brash and garish in her look. She had draped herself in bright, flowing clothes that were arresting but verged on theatrical. The huge, wide-brimmed hat that she had topped the creation off with would have been a step too far for a less attractive woman but Ava's sparkly blue eyes and broad, ready grin meant that the overall effect was 'kookie' and adorable. The two women did manage to complement each other in a strange way and it was difficult not to gaze at both of them. Not that the man interviewing them was trying to disguise the fact that he could not take his eyes off them.

The hulking German sat behind his mahogany desk, taking regular totes of a cigarette. The smell of it was acrid, but partly diluted by the pleasant smell coming from by the bubbling coffee in the percolator at his side. He wore a white suit that clung in all the wrong places to his frame. The sleeves rode too high up his wrists and the buttons on his brown shirt strained across his tummy. Although not a young man, he had an impressive head of thick hair, dyed brown but showing distinctly ginger at the roots as the morning sun streamed into the office. His face was animated with a broad grin as his eyes darting admiringly from one woman to the other. Humbert Mueller was the sole employee of the London office, reporting directly to Rosie and Reiman Shultz-Klopper in Hanover. He was responsible for scouting and booking and spent his evenings scouring every chorus line in every show to spot fresh, promising and (above all) inexpensive new talent.

'I must say, my dears, you look even more beautiful than you did on stage! Such a great show!'

Although German born, Mueller had barely a trace of an accent and, if anything, had acquired a little bit of a Cockney twang after fifteen years in London.

'So, Mr Mueller-' Satine began.

'Ah, Humbert, please!'

'So, Humbert,' Satine began again, adjusting the lapels of her bolero jacket so that they were covering a little more of her blouse in a vain attempt to stop the Mueller from staring at her chest. 'You want us to fly out to Germany to audition for a new pop group?' Satine was trying to be as upbeat as possible, but the very mention of flying was giving her a sense of dread. She had never been on a plane before, and it was not a situation she was in any hurry to change. Nevertheless, Ava had waxed lyrical about the potential of the audition that she had secured them and, Satine had to admit, it was more appealing than the thought of another chorus gig.

'The Shultz-Kloppers are not just starting a new group, my dears,' Mueller leaning across the table, his eyes sparkling. 'They are going to create a group that will turn the world on its head! Cutting edge pop from the best of the German producers. Knockout disco floor-filler hits. And the most beautiful singers!'

Ava giggled at this, clearly lost in the rapture of Mueller's excited hype. Ever the pragmatist, Satine continued:

'What about audition tapes? I mean, we can sing. We sing really well! But don't they want proof of that before we make the trip?' Ava shot her a cold look at this, thinking that blind enthusiasm was the order of the day. However, the question did not seem to bother Mueller at all. He extinguished his cigarette, promptly lighting another and chuckled:

'You both sounded good to me. Why question it?'

'Hard to pick out individual voices in a chorus, though.' Satine was not going to be mollified so easily, even though this statement won her a sharp kick in the ankle from Ava.

'This is the 1970s! You wouldn't believe the wizardry that they have now. The Shultz-Klopper sound machine can make a crow sound like Streisand – not that I think it will be an issue with you two talented ladies! Besides, you have,' he paused and made another shameless sweep of both of the women's figures with his beady eyes, 'quite the look that we need.'

'Not many mixed girl bands out there – none actually.' This observation came from Ava. Satine smiled. She could underestimate her friend at times, but this was a very valid question. Fear of flying aside, Germany was a long way to go just to be told that they the Shultz-Kloppers were going in another direction. Or, worse still for the friends, that one of them (the white one) was deemed more suitable than the other.

'Exactly and regrettably so.' Mueller's reply was reassuringly frank. 'And we think that it is time to do something about that. Hence the name – Mixed Emotions. It works on many levels.'

Mixed Emotions.' Satine repeated the words, liking how they sounded. She looked at Ava and smiled. Speaking for them both, she said:

'When do we go?'

The wait for the end of the run in the musical seemed endless in the wake of their meeting with Mueller. Satine and Ava had scoured every music press article they could find on the Shultz-Kloppers. In the mornings before matinee performances, Satine had got in the habit of frequenting the nearest library to their bedsit, scouring the microfilmed records of old newspapers. Pickings were slim as the Shultz-Klopper phenomenon had not really impacted on the British scene. There had been two singles that had dented the top forty charts and gone down well in the clubs. One had been called 'Deeper in Love' and was supposedly performed by a group or perhaps solo artist called 'Tiffany Laverne.' Satine could find no actual record of this artist existing, either as a singer or group outfit. The second, marginally more successful single had been released under the name of 'Summer Fever' and was called 'Hot Holiday Love.' The singer sounded remarkably like the elusive Tiffany Laverne, and Satine came to the conclusion that both tracks had been performed by the same session singer or singers. This did not trouble her greatly – she knew that this was becoming an increasing phenomenon. Perhaps the Shultz-Klopper hit machine was looking to make the leap to having an identifiable group. Certainly, the idea of being part of a racially integrated concept thrilled her but there was also the nagging doubt that this trip (via a dreaded plane ride) might be an elaborate session singing gig that would soon see them fade into oblivion along with Tiffany Laverne and Summer Fever. Ava, typically, had dismissed what she called Satine's 'bad vibes' and focused on the fact that the trip was paid for and would be an experience if nothing else. Satine had to agree, especially when the only other work option that had come up was a tour of working men's club doing covers of Motown hits. The pay would have been terrible and, from experience, she knew that the accommodation offered in provincial towns would be even worse.

Finally, the two women were free to fly out to Hanover. Their dour landlady had been surprisingly helpful in advising them that they would find their destination colder than London and, dragging bags bursting with hastily purchased winter clothes, Satine and Ava arrived at London Heathrow. Having checked in, the two bedded into high stools by a worktop counter and sipped warm gin and tonics.

'Exciting, isn't it!' Ava cooed, looking at the departures board above them that rattled out the names of forthcoming flights to far flung locations.

'Yes,' Satine replied after a few moments.

'Tell your face, then!'

'Sorry,' Satine shivered as she spoke, 'but I can't think past the journey. I'm terrified.'

'Did you take those herbal pills?'

'Yes – at least four! I'm hoping the gin will get them started.' Ava reached out and squeezed Satine's hand. The two stared into each other's eyes for a few moments, each drawing comfort from the other's presence.

'Uhu.' Satine pointed up at the departure board, a section of which had just rattled around to spell out the Hanover flight and the now open departure gate. She swigged back the contents of her glass. Smiling, Ava passed the half- filled glass she had been holding to Satine. Satine dutifully drained the second glass, feeling the warm burn and immediate sense of heaviness in her legs as she stood up. Without further word, the two women made their way to their departure gate. They were first to arrive, with a snaking line of fellow passengers rapidly forming behind them.

Elsewhere in the airport, the Interpol agent stubbed out his cigarette and stared intently at the woman. In his eight years of experience in the role, he had to admit that he had rarely encountered such a cool customer as the woman who sat across the table from him. The deliberately sparse room was kept uncomfortably cold in winter and stiflingly hot in the summer, designed to exacerbate the desire to be allowed to go and speed up the talking process. Yet, although she had wrapped her chilled hands around the plastic cup of coffee she had requested, he noticed that she had not touched any of the liquid that was now, surely, stone cold.

'So, let's just go over this one more time.' The agent glanced at the small grey clock on the otherwise empty wall of the interview room. Following his gaze, the woman nodded.

'I would appreciate if it were for the *last* time, officer.' She spoke in the same annoyingly calm tone. 'My flight is likely to have been called by now.'

'If you don't mind..' The agent managed to keep his rising annoyance in check. He knew that he had no reason to keep her now. If she missed her flight, it would be he who would be facing questions from his superiors. There would be nothing to follow up, not even the smallest reason to even suggest that the woman report to one of his colleagues once she arrived in Germany. Yet, for all this, the agent was troubled. Something about the woman did not add up. A gut instinct told him that she knew more than she was telling. Her poise was faultless, but every now and again he saw a glimmer of something in her eye when he mentioned certain names and places. Paris. Philippe Le Grande. Not a *reaction* as such; she was too good for that. But there was a shadow that seemed to move across her, especially when Le Grande's name was spoken. To that end, he had kept mentioning both it and Paris frequently throughout the hour she had been in the room. But, as if aware that she was betraying something, the woman had seemed to hold whatever it was in check after a while. Now, the words seemed to provoke nothing except a hint of boredom. There was something that nagged at the man, like a glimpse of a figure in the corner of the eye that turned out not to be there but left a lingering doubt.

'I have indeed lived and worked in Paris, albeit briefly.' If the woman was anxious about her flight, she kept it in check and her tone was as mild as ever. 'I had no fixed address as I crashed on the sofas of various acquaintances for the duration. I can supply you with names, but I don't really remember the addresses. I could make a guess.'

'Totalling four weeks?'

'Three weeks and three days.'

'Singing at a club owned by Philippe Le Grande. The same Philippe Le Grande whose remains were found in the burned-out wreck of a flat above a bar to which he had seemingly no connection.'

'Yes. And the woman drummed her finger on the table top to emphasise her words as she spoke, 'I had no direct contact with him whilst I was in Paris and I only knew he had died when you told me.'

'And you had no reason to suspect that this man had connections to organised crime? Nobody warned you off?'

'It was, as I have said, a good opportunity.' The woman stared at him levelly. 'In my profession, it is never a good idea to turn down work without a good reason. It also pays not to ask too many questions. If …this man was a criminal, he would not be the first to finance a club from dubious sources. He won't be the last. I did the work, collected my pay and moved on to the next booking. It was Amsterdam afterwards, if you must know. A festival.'

The agent had not missed the pause as the woman seemed to decide not to say Le Grande's name. Was she afraid that she would betray something in her tone? But he knew that he had reached a dead end. The legal limit of time in which he could detain her without a formal charge had expired – they both knew that.

 Minutes later, the woman was gone. The agent stared down at the manilla folder on his lap. He filed the notes he had made in the folder and slid it into his briefcase. With frustration, he snapped the catches shut on the briefcase and left the room.

Satine was only aware that she was clutching the safety belt buckle when Ava pointed out that they were still on the ground. She tried to relax her grip and Ava did a reasonable job of distracting her by appraising the quality of the male passengers that emerged from the doorway and made their way past as they looked for their seats. There had been a couple of stunningly handsome men, clearly German with their beautiful blond hair and strong jaws. This made both women optimistic as to the potential local flavour of their destination. There was a poise, a relaxed elegance about European men that did not seem to extend to the British. It was a quiet confidence, a refreshing self-assurance that was not common amongst British males. European men seemed happy to groom themselves without the fear that the average British man had that they would be labelled a 'poof' and likened to comedian Larry Grayson or even Danny La Rue if they were too neat or even too clean! The late afternoon flight was now almost full, and from their position at the front of the passenger compartment, they could see the cabin crew beginning their preparations. Indeed, the steady stream of passengers had slowed to a trickle and, in the recent minutes, nobody had emerged from the doorway. This made the sudden appearance of the last passenger all the more striking: tall, willowy and with radiantly glowing brown skin, the woman was immaculately dressed in a tailored suit. Her hair was hidden by a beige turban that seemed to accentuate the beautifully angled cheekbones of her face.

Although she was clearly running late for the flight, Satine could not help noticing the poise of the woman that made her entrancing. She made her way towards the rear of the plane, locking eyes with Satine briefly as she glided past her with a look that was not unkind. The brief show of recognition of another person of colour should not have been necessary or comforting, yet it still was, and Satine had not failed to observe that the woman was only the fifth non-white passenger that had boarded, herself included.

One of the cabin crew immediately bolted the huge sliding door of the plane as soon as the captivating woman had disappeared from their view, and Ava gave Satine a quick peck on her cheek.

'Here's to the future!' Ava grinned at Satine, willing her to focus on what was to come at the end of their journey and not the fact that she would soon be miles above the ground in a metal tube with no control over her fate. Satine managed a tight smile, but found that her hands had tightened around the seat buckle again.

By the time they reached Hanover, Satine's palms would be bruised in a perfectly square indentation of the buckle that would not fade for a week.

Chapter Two – City of Dreams?

Dusk was descending along with the plane and, by the time the two women had reclaimed their baggage and exited the terminal at Hanover, it was night in the city. Relief at having survived the flight was short lived for Satine as she gazed at the industrialised panorama that was Hanover. In her imagination, she had anticipated quaintly shuttered windows dressing whitewashed houses and pine forest enshrouded mountains behind them as far as the eye could see. Instead, the slate grey vista comprised factories, office buildings and looked remarkably like the city she had just left albeit on a smaller scale.

'Not what I had in mind,' Satine shivered as she tightened her coat about her torso and turned up the collar. An icy wind bit into her cheeks and added to the sense of gloom that she was trying her best to chase away. As ever, Ava was more upbeat:

'No city looks its best from the pavement outside an airport. Besides, they told us we were staying outside the city itself. It's bound to be prettier in the suburbs. Now…where's our ride?'

Both women began to scan the bustling mass of people that were making their way either into or away from the terminal building. A taxi rank to their left was a hive of activity as luggage was loaded and new arrivals ferried away. They had been told that someone would meet them upon arrival and drive them to the accommodation that had been arranged. A rapidly diminishing clutch of people held up pieces of cardboard or paper with surnames written on them, as one by one the arrivals found their drivers. Satine and Ava scanned the faces and signs hopefully, but there did not seem to be anyone holding the legend 'Lancaster and Simone' aloft.

After a time, Satine noticed a strange figure leaning against a car that had been parked at an alarming angle a few yards away from the taxi rank. The vehicle looked like it had been abandoned rather than parked with any sense of proximity to the pavement. Equally, the driver had clearly taken the 'strictly no waiting' sign printed in several languages as a joke. The figure leaning against the aforementioned vehicle was holding a piece of paper in their hand, but it was pointed downwards and Satine could not make out the writing on it. As if sensing that Satine was trying to see the paper, the figure suddenly titled it upwards and it caught the light of an overhead streetlamp. Lancashire and Simon. Close enough.

'That's us! That car over there. That…man has our names. Well, almost.'

Satine had hesitated as she identified the figure's gender. The man was tall, with cropped iron-grey hair that stood poker straight in a GI Joe style. His jaw was square, yet there was a dainty softness about the mouth and a cupid's bow shape to the lips that belied the angular, stern bone structure. Satine waved at the man and he raised his hand in response, not smiling at all but flashing acknowledgement in his eyes. The eyes! Satine could not quite put a finger on it, but there was something in the glassy green eyes that seemed both hostile and mysterious.

The two women approached the man and Ava spoke:

'Hi! Are you our ride? We're Ava and Satine, for the Shultz-Kloppers.'

The man smiled suddenly and broadly at Ava. Satine noticed just how green and pretty his eyes were. Then, in an instant, the man flashed those eyes away from Ava and looked directly at Satine. The smile evaporated and his lantern jaw seemed to tighten.

'Welcome to Hanover.'

The voice was rich, strongly accented but not as deep as either woman was expecting. Satine knew that the welcome was not really extended to both of them. She felt the uncomfortable prickle of hostility in the man's demeanour. Satine had scanned the crowds in the airport and outside, noticing that Hanover's population seemed much whiter in composition than London. The hostility she detected did not necessarily surprise, but it always disappointed and hurt.

'I'm Ava. This is Satine,' Ava continued brightly, not missing the shift in attitude the man had displayed but deciding not to make anything of it at this point. Satine knew her friend well enough to know that she would not stay quiet if the man's attitude remained biased against her and was not upset at Ava's approach to the man.

'I am Katrinka Weiler.' The man paused, almost as if her expected that name to mean something to the two women. It didn't, but both were immediately struck by how melodic and somehow inappropriate the first name sounded when matched to the brusque figure of Mr Weiler. 'You will be staying in an apartment in my building for your stay here.'

Great, thought Satine. Mrs S had been a harpy, but she was not in prejudiced in any manner. Satine forced herself to smile at Weiler, which he returned briefly this time. However, Satine noticed that the smile never reached those green eyes.

'Shall we put our bags in?' Satine ventured, determined that she was not going to make it easy for him.

'Oh, allow me!' Weiler said these words with the sentiment of 'fuck you' but took the bags from both women and loaded the car.

Twenty minutes later, Satine and Ava were relieved to gaze upon much prettier surroundings as Weiler drove them out of the city centre. The grey, industrial sprawl slowly receded and the commercial buildings gave way to homes, grass verges running parallel to the highway now lined with trees. There were even some of the shutters that Satine imagined, although there was a fair amount of newly built property along the wide avenues that they now travelled along. Weiler had not engaged them in much conversation and the women found themselves drowsy as they rested on the back seats of the warm and very impressive Mercedes. Neither were particularly enthusiastic about cars, with London life meaning that owning one was not really an issue. But they liked the smell of money and success that Weiler's car gave out! Just as Satine found herself drifting into a welcome doze, the car pulled off the road and onto a small driveway. They had reached their new home.

The building itself had clearly been a single residency when it had been built but had been subsequently divided into apartments. The façade of the building was faded and chipped stucco, but the former glory of the building still remained in the beautiful carved features around the window and door frames. It looked to be several hundred years old and both women were immediately impressed by its effortless grandeur. Weiler conducted them to the second floor of the building, insisting that he would get their bags later in a display of chivalry that added another layer of confusion to the opinion the women were forming of their host. The apartment was big and open-plan in its layout. To Ava and Satine, used to London spaces, it seemed vast. The décor was minimalist and tasteful, quite masculine but with a few touches that softened the overall effect and added a sense of welcoming. The lair of Weiler, Satine mused. Much nicer than she had expected, and, like the car, the place was reassuringly high end and reflected success.

Both women were particularly excited to see a telephone hanging from a mount on the wall of the kitchen area.

Without having to be asked, Weiler had told them that they could, indeed, use the phone to call relatives in England but were to please do so only once a week and limit their calls to five minutes. The bill came to him and was fully itemised, he added joylessly.

'This is beautiful!' Ava cooed, twirling around in the centre of the lounge area. Satine's eyes fell on a black and white photograph that hung above the large fireplace in the centre of a wall of exposed, white-washed brick. The picture was of a beautiful, naked African woman. As she looked away, she noticed that Weiler had followed her gaze and knew she had been looking at the image.

'That's a beautiful picture. Who took it?' Awkwardness had prompted the question but it had been mixed with genuine curiosity.

'It is my work.'

'Who is the woman? She's beautiful.' This came from Ava, which made Satine feel less uncomfortable.

'She was…is beautiful,' Weiler replied, sounding unexpectedly vulnerable in the face of Ava's question. 'A lost love.' Those three words were said very quietly, and for a few moments Weiler gazed at the picture as if he had never seen it before, almost as if trying to access a memory that seemed beyond him. Satine, initially certain that Weiler's hostility had been racism, was now confused. Perhaps Weiler had just taken an instant dislike to her and was not prejudiced. In time, Satine would not waste time grieving over whether strangers liked her or not, but her youthful innocence made her easily wounded and she suddenly felt the distance of every mile they had travelled. Her eyes went to the telephone and she reassured herself that she would soon be able to hear her mother's voice.

Weiler coughed awkwardly and made his way to the door. He stood on the threshold for a few moments, saying:

'There are two sets of keys in a bowl by the fridge. One for the main door, the other for the apartment. I am directly below, so I would appreciate as much quiet as you can manage. I have stocked the fridge and the cupboards and that should last you for a few days at least.'

'You have been so kind,' Ava managed and was repaid by an alarmingly genuine grin from Weiler. Satine found herself thinking that maybe she was the lucky one for not being liked. Ava was certainly going down a storm. 'I didn't notice any shops. Is there a supermarket or something nearby – maybe a pharmacy?'

Weiler provided directions for both stores and closed the door behind him. Ava went immediately to the fridge and was pleasantly surprised to see that the provisions Weiler had stocked up on for them included two bottles of white wine. Locating two glasses, Ava insisted that they made a toast to their future success. Mueller had appraised them of the itinerary for their trip and both women knew that the first night would be free of activities and they could, therefore, settle back and recover from their journey.

'He certainly likes you,' Satine teased as they curled up on the matching white leather sofas.

'You, not so much! I thought it was a colour thing, but –' she waved her glass at the portrait above the fireplace.

'My thoughts exactly. Odd…guy.' Satine frowned. Once again, she found that words did not seem to come easily where Weiler was concerned. There was something about him that words just did not seem to cover.

Ava decided to take a long bath before bed after they had finished one of the bottles of wine, but Satine felt she needed some air before retiring. Remembering Weiler's directions, she walked briskly towards the late night supermarket that occupied the corner unit of a building that was only about three hundred yards from the apartment.

The wine had lowered her body temperature and Satine huddled into her coat as she walked into the icy breeze that whipped around the tall buildings. There were few people around, a few cafés and bars dotted here and there glowed invitingly but this was not really a commercial area. As she walked past the residential buildings that flanked the pavement she could see the familiar blue glow of television set light filling windows. Most people were settled in for the evening. Satine was impressed by the tidiness of the streets. The litter and graffiti of London was not replicated here and there was a sense of order that should have been reassuring. However, Satine found that the lack of detritus only reminded her more that she was a long way from home. She had wanted to call her mother that evening, but decided to wait until she thought she could be more positive. Her mother had not wanted her to take the offer, that was clear. She hadn't said so, naturally, but there had been a tightness in her voice and a few too many silences the last time they had spoken. Staunchly supportive of her endeavours to make a success, Satine's mother always walked a line between showing enthusiasm and masking her fears for her daughter's safety. No, the first call home would be best left for a few days.

As Satine entered the small, but mercifully warm supermarket she noticed that there were only a few customers. Two men, both tall and blonde like so many of the passengers on the plane, were making their way out of the shop as she arrived. Both stared at her appreciatively, making her feel self-conscious but in a much more pleasant manner than Weiler had done.

An older woman with grey hair and glasses sat behind a counter near the rear of the shop. Satine smiled at her, buoyant from the admiring glances she had just received from the two men. The woman gazed blankly back at her before lowering her eyes to return to the magazine she was flicking through. Having obtained the few items she wanted, Satine stood a few yards from the woman, awaiting acknowledgement to move forwards to be served. The woman looked up and over Satine's shoulder, nodding. The recipient of the nod, a young blonde woman, stepped in front of Satine, knocking her shoulder as she did so in a manner that Satine knew was meant. The older woman smiled and chatted with the customer, who gave Satine a defiant look as she exited the shop. With no sense of shame for the blatant snub, the older woman gestured for Satine to place her items on the counter. Satine's attempts to use the German phrases she had learned garnered no encouragement and the woman snatched the money from Satine as she extended her hand, dropping her change onto the counter without a word.

Satine had put a brave face on when she returned to the apartment, telling Ava that the local shop was perfectly well stocked and easy to find. She took a shower and then sat on the sofa for a long time after Ava had gone to bed, watching the television with the sound off and periodically glancing longingly at the phone on the wall.

Exhaustion rather than peace had taken Satine into a deep and dreamless sleep. She awoke to the sound of the radio blaring in the kitchen area and the clattering of pots and pans. Noticing that light was only just starting to creep into the room via the gaps around the heavy curtains, she fumbled for her wristwatch that was on the small night stand by her side. 7am. Since when did Ava become an early bird? Much less fix breakfast! Or, indeed, eat breakfast save for about three industrial strength coffees that looked like they had spouted from a Texas oilrig. Locating her robe, Satine hastily dragged her hair from out of her eyes, tying it back in a haphazard chignon before padding off barefooted towards the cacophony of noise outside the bedroom.

Satine was greeted by the sight of Ava, as tousled and semi-awake as she felt herself to be, slumped at the breakfast bar that separated the kitchen from the lounge area. Behind her stood a stranger, whisking a bowl of eggs. The shells of four eggs lay scattered on the worktop. A large saucepan coated in melted butter steamed on the electric hob. At the sight of Satine, the figure quickly poured the eggs into the pan and picked up a coffee mug. She poured it full with delightfully aromatic smelling coffee from a pot that simmered next to the saucepan. Holding the mug out towards Satine, the figure shouted:

'Ah! Satine, you are awake too! Good!'

Satine stepped forward and accepted the mug, catching Ava's eye as she did so and both women exchanged equally bemused looks.

'Er,' Satine began, 'thanks but –'

'Rosie Shultz-Klopper, apparently.' Ava whispered. Satine blinked herself into proper wakefulness as she sipped the ultra-strong but delicious coffee that she had been given. The woman had assumed correctly that, like Ava, she took her coffee black. The strength was a little too much for Satine's usual taste, but it helped sharpen her focus on the figure in the kitchen. Rosie Shultz-Klopper had now turned

41

her back to them and was feverishly whisking the eggs as they began to scramble. With her free hand, she pushed the lever down on a four-slot toaster that resided on the counter. Satine slipped onto a stool beside Ava and whispered:

'Did you let her in?'

'God, no! First thing I knew about it was the clattering! She has her own key, apparently. They all do.' Ava frowned as she said this, and both women shared the sense of vulnerability. The dawning thought that they may have signed on to something very odd would not go away for either of them. Satine could hear her mother's voice giving the sage warning about things that seemed too good to be true. The toaster pinged and seconds later Rosie Shultz-Klopper placed two plates of perfectly scrambled eggs and toast before them. Both stared at the plates, still trying to process what was going on.

'Eat! Eat! Long day for you girls today. And I don't make a habit of cooking for people - so eat!' The strange figure barked. The accent was softer that Weiler's and the English perfect. Satine wondered how much German she would pick up if everyone she met spoke English so well, but she managed a smile and a polite murmuring of thanks as she gazed at the woman, who was now at least keeping still. She was not tall by any means, but had a presence that belied her diminutive stature. Her age was difficult to guess at as she had white hair but skin that was without a wrinkle. There was a tautness of the skin around the eyes and cheeks that Satine thought had been achieved by surgical assistance. The woman's skin had a sheen and tightness to it that she had noticed on women who sat in the best and most expensive seats in the audience of the theatres back home. She has once been in the chorus of a show that featured a legend from the Hollywood era. The woman, seventy if she was a day, had a similarly flawless and translucent quality about her face. Satine had stood behind the screen icon in the wings just before the start of the second act each night of the run and had become fascinated by the little scars that she glimpsed behind the woman's ears. Conscious that she was staring, Satine ventured conversation:

'This is lovely, Mrs-'

'Just Rosie will do! My, but you too are pretty! Mueller chose you well,' the woman grinned broadly at this and Satine was almost dazzled by the whiteness and perfect alignment of Rosie's teeth. She remembered the clacking horse dentures of Mrs S and wondered if these too were false teeth, albeit extremely expensive ones. 'Now, eat up! I'll leave you to tidy up afterwards,' Rosie gestured vaguely at the debris she had left in the kitchen. With that, she picked up a very expensive looking handbag that had been placed on the breakfast bar and was halfway to the door. Without turning back she shouted:

'Frau Weiler will take you to the studio at nine. No photos today, but S.K. likes his girls to look glamorous so don't scrimp on the warpaint!' With that, she was gone.

'Guess that was Rosie!' Ava announced, taking her plate of untouched eggs and toast over to the silver pedal bin and scraping them away. She poured herself another coffee and sauntered back to her bedroom, saying she needed another half an hour and that Satine could use the bathroom first.

Weiler blasted the horn of the Mercedes at precisely 9am from where he sat, revving the engine on the street just outside the apartment building. Dressed in her typically stylish and Spanish-influenced manner, Satine had swept her hair back into a neat ponytail and had matched her bright red nails to her lipstick. Otherwise, her make-up was subtle and the overall look was of understated glamour and quite natural. Ava had, as expected, taken Rosie's challenge onboard with aplomb. She had blow-dried her long tresses into a floaty, pre-Raphaelite mane and wore a fitted white dress that flared out at her hips. Her long, willowy legs were flashed to spectacular effect as she walked, owing to two long slits in the dress. Her eyes were thick with mascara to an extent that would have made Liza Minnelli look like a mole.

'Good morning!' Satine forced herself to call brightly as she slipped into the back of the car. Weiler made no reply, but when Ava made a similar statement she received a little wave. Fuck you then, Satine decided. She had not missed the fact that Rosie had called him 'Frau Weiler' earlier on, and she spent a large part of the twenty minute journey trying to get a better look at her driver's face in the rear-view mirror as they sped along the busy streets that took them back into the centre of Hanover. But the jaw was just as square and manly as she had remembered it from the night before.

The studio itself was nothing to look at from the street. Indeed, the building looked like many other bland two story commercial units on the semi-industrial estate that they had been taken to by Weiler. He had deposited them on the pavement without ceremony, speeding off as soon as they had clambered out of the car.

two-story'Charming as ever,' Satine snarled after the departing vehicle.

'Fuck him.' Ava's succinct comment echoed Satine's thoughts perfectly and the two women smiled at each other. Wordlessly, they both turned to look at the façade of the building. Above a smart but unremarkable red door was a large sign that proclaimed ' Shultz-Klopper's Music World.' They squeezed each other's hands tightly, the sign seeming to make sense of everything in an instant. This was what it had all been about.

'Come in, girls!' The door flew open and Rosie stood before them. She had changed from the jeans and box jacket combo she had been wearing that morning and was now resplendent in a black catsuit and beret. A chunky necklace glinted as several large diamonds caught the sunlight. She looked Satine and Ava up and down slowly and without any obvious concern as to whether she was making them uncomfortable.

'Mm,' she mused at length, 'quite different styles going on with you two girls.'

'Is that…okay?' Satine ventured, feeling more self-conscious (as usual) than Ava. If Rosie should have taken this as a cue to stop staring, she ignored it. She did not answer Satine for what seemed a small eternity. Then, just when it seemed she was not going to say anything at all, Rosie broke into the broad, dazzlingly bleached grin again and said:

'I like it! Gives a sense that there are different personalities going on in the group. Maybe you could lengthen your hair.' This last thought was directed at Satine. 'Do you have wigs?'

More than a little offended at the question itself and the bluntness of its delivery, Satine prickled:

'I can't stand to wear wigs! I can do a lot of different styles with my own hair. Why, is it a problem?'

Something like surprise flashed in Rosie's eyes for a moment, but she nodded slowly and then said:

'No. No problem. Anyway, come on! In you come! S.K. is waiting upstairs.' Hardly reassured, the two women followed Rosie past a small reception area and headed towards a narrow stairwell. There was a row of chairs against the window in the reception area. A receptionist sat

47

at her desk, talking into a telephone and writing down a message onto a small pad. On one of the chairs sat a young man. He looked up as the group walked by, catching Satine's eye and smiling shyly. He was probably about Satine's age, she thought, with white blonde hair and a cute face. He reminded her of Adam Faith and he had the same sparkly blue eyes. But Rosie was cracking quite a pace, and Satine and Ava were soon scurrying up the stairs after her and the cute young man was lost from view.

When Ava and Satine had attended auditions before, they had all tended to merge into a similar pattern. Rows of hopeful auditionees would stand or sit in line, waiting to get their three minutes to perform. There would usually be a small band, certainly a pianist if nothing else and their judges would scrutinise them as they sat on an intimidating panel, usually in the stalls if the audition was in a theatre. The studio they stood in was not like anything they had encountered before. For a start, there were no musical instruments to be seen, not even a small keyboard tucked in a corner. The room resembled something out of Star Trek, with panels of mixing boards and large tape spools on the walls. One corner of the room was occupied by a recording booth. No bigger than a phone box, it had glass panels on each side and a microphone hanging from the ceiling in its centre.

 In the midst of the array of mixing desks sat a toad of a man. He was bulky, with a face that was stern and full of experience. A scar ran the length of his left cheek and stopped just below his eye. The eyes themselves were deep set, dark and watchful. His hair was scraped back from an expansive forehead and tied neatly at the nape of his neck in a tiny little pigtail. He wore a black suit that was clearly expensively cut despite the way it seemed to strain under the pressure of its inhabitant. A huge cigar was wedged between two of his thick fingers and its foul stench filled the room. He peered at the two women for a long time, barely blinking. Used to being stared at as they were by now, both Ava and Satine found this scrutiny the most unsettling they could recall. The man had a way of looking through as well as at someone and it seemed his mind was constantly racing to his own private conclusions. Eventually, Reiman Shultz-Klopper spoke. When he did, it was a guttural growl of a voice and all in German. He directed his words to Rosie but his eyes never left Ava and Satine. Rosie replied to S.K. and there were further exchanges of words, all in German. Eventually, Rosie turned to the two women and said:

'S.K. thinks you look terrific! Just the right image for Mixed Emotions.'

S.K. nodded at each word, indicating that he understood English perfectly well even thought he was not going to speak it. Nice trick, thought Satine. Clearly, S.K. enjoyed powerplays. However, Satine noticed that at least now the big man was smiling at them. The smile faded automatically after a few seconds and it was clear that S.K. was deep in thought again.

'We have prepared audition pieces.' Ava directed this at Rosie. Rosie looked towards S.K. and the two conversed again. Satine could pick out some of the words they were saying, but the rapidity of the native speaker does not ever lend itself to being followed successfully by someone who is only just learning a new language.

'S.K. would like to hear you sing.' Rosie directed this to Satine. Ava and Satine exchanged puzzled glances, but Satine quickly recovered and replied:

'Sure thing! Do you want me to –'

'Step into the sound booth. S.K. has all the instrumentation he needs on his desk. Just your voice will do today.' Rosie motioned Satine towards the booth and she stepped inside it and closed the door, grateful that the interior had been protected from the vile smell of S.K.'s cigar. She looked out at S.K. who was sliding dials up and down on the mixing desk. A huge tape spool on the wall started to revolve. Rosie leaned into a microphone on the mixing desk and soon Satine could hear her voice coming from speakers within the sound booth, which was disorientating at first.

'Put on the headphones that are hanging on the wall, and in your own time, let's have the first verse and chorus of something.'

'what would you like? I have several different tempos I could-'

'Anything will do. What's your favourite of the songs you have prepared? Something modern.'

'Er,' Satine quickly made up her mind that she would treat them to a rendition of one of the tunes from the musical they had been in that had soared up the charts when made into a single with a dance beat. Rosie nodded and, moments later Satine was purring through the first verse before belting out the chorus. Getting into her stride rapidly, she began to intone the start of the second verse when S.K. shouted something at Rosie. Satine floundered, dropping to silence immediately.

'S.K. says that is great! All we need.'

Bemused, Satine hung up the headphones and stepped out of the sound booth. Ava walked towards her, smiling enthusiastically before taking up her place in the booth and putting on the headphones in preparation for her own audition. Although not a naturally talented singer like Satine, Ava was confident that she could deliver a tune competently and it seemed that the audition itself was a breeze if Satine's brief trial was anything to go by. However, no sooner had Ava took up position in the booth than S.K. started shouting at Rosie. Placating him expertly, Rosie stalked over to the sound booth and opened the door.

'That's not necessary,' Rosie snapped, taking Ava none too gently by the arm and pulling her out of the booth. Ava scarcely had time to remove the headphones and prevent herself from being bounced back into the booth by their flex. She smoothed her hair self-consciously and stood close to Satine, both women instinctively holding hands in silent solidarity.

'Is there something wrong?' Ava asked, her eyes moving from between S.K. and Rosie. S.K. just looked down at his mixing desk, but Rosie flashed the nuclear blast smile again:

'Wrong? How could anything be wrong? S.K. is more than happy – with both of you!'

'But-' Ava began but was cut off by the sound of S.K. barking something else at Rosie. Rosie nodded and then turned back to Satine and Ava.

'All is good! Now, we have to be getting along with the club.'

Chapter Three – Champagne for Everyone!

Klub Kasbah was no worse than most nightclubs of its type, Satine decided. It only looked and smelled so awful because it was still morning, and the lights were on fully. There was no pulsing music to drown out the ear-splitting sound of the two bar staff throwing empty bottles into a large plastic skip; the tears and stains on the velvet booths and the scratches on the circular table tops were not hidden under the ambient lighting that would typically wave a wand of glamour; the smells rising from the damp and sticky carpet was not masked by the perfume and cigarettes that would hide the staler (if not necessarily better) odour from the gallons of spilled drinks. In many ways, the club could have been any one of the similarly seedy establishments in London, apart from one perturbing feature: on a large expanse of wall there was a projector screen, onto which was being displayed a somewhat grainy but unmistakably graphic film of a couple having sex. The sound level was mercifully low, but Satine could still hear the soundtrack of gasps, guttural moans and the twanging and off-key musical non-diegetics. Both Ava and Satine were transfixed by the screen and its uncensored images. There were plenty of sex shops around Soho in London,

54

certainly, but they were all shrouded in blacked out windows and doors. Their neon signs enticed the curious with promises of 'XXX' films and magazines, but there was nothing else to be seen from the streets. Ava giggled as the scene before them reached an obvious climax (in every sense of the word) but Satine found herself looking at the stained carpets and felt increasingly uncomfortable. She had also noticed that the dance floor itself had three raised areas – clearly podiums for individual dancers. The type of dancing that was done on these podiums, (if the nature of the films was anything to go by), was hardly likely to be anything other than striptease. Following her eye-line, Ava whispered:

'And I thought we would just be singing for our supper!'

Before she had chance to reply, Satine found herself being guided by the arm to move forward by Rosie. The woman had maintained the same upbeat, friendly but ultimately patronising demeanour that had been served up with their eggs and toast in the morning.

'S.K. will expect you girls to spend at least four nights a week working here while we set everything up.' She waved her arm out to in the direction of the booths.

'Doing what exactly?!' Satine did not try to hide the dismay in her voice. Rosie stared at her and grinned:

'Nothing I would not or have not done myself! We are not Bluebeards!' She motioned the women to sit in one of the nearest booths and slid beside them. She leaned on her elbows, dropped her voice and spoke to them in a tone that she clearly hoped was reassuring. It failed spectacularly if this aim, and she sounded more like the a Bond villain.

'S.K. invests a lot of time and money in his projects. There are huge costs for the publicity, the photo shoots, getting on radio playlists – the list goes on and on! We need you to generate some income to help with all that while we get Mixed Emotions off the ground. You see?'

'We do,' Satine stared levelly at Rosie as she spoke, 'but we are not anyone's pieces of meat!'

Satine looked at Ava to see if she was going to add anything. Although Ava nodded at her, she refrained from saying anything to endorse what Satine had said.

'Ah! I think you have leapt to some unfortunate…conclusions about Klub Kasbah.' Rosie flashed the impossible straight, white teeth again. Now, Satine was more inclined to picture a shark than a rich socialite. Not for the first time, she noticed that the smile did not reach Rosie's eyes.

'Hard not to reach conclusions when you look at the onscreen entertainment, Rosie.'

'Ah,' Rosie shrugged, 'not to my taste either, but all pretty harmless fun. I think you will find Germany a little, shall we say, more easy going than the UK where that sort of thing is concerned. But that is not to say you will find us immoral. The work we wish you to do will take place here,' she tapped the table, 'and here only.'

'Go on.' This time it was Ava who spoke, much to Satine's relief. Her silence up until now had started to concern Satine.

'We have many gentleman customers who like the company and conversation of pretty young women. *Just* company and conversation. They will not be allowed to overstep the mark at any point. There will be many eyes on you at all times – including mine.' Neither woman was quite sure if the last words were meant to be reassuring or a warning.

'Just talking?' Satine was not convinced, and in no mood to hide her doubt.

'Talking and…making sure they spend their money. If they spend time with you, they will know that you like champagne. We have plenty of champagne.'

'Let me guess,' Ava said, 'champagne that will cost them a lot more per bottle than it cost to stock in the first place. A lot more?'

'But, of course. The longer they spend with you, the more you will expect them to pour the champagne.' Rosie leaned forwards and whispered –'champagne that you will quite often find you spill whilst laughing at their jokes. Nes pas?'

Before either Satine or Ava could comment further, their attention was taken by a new arrival in the room. Looking as captivating as she had when they first set eyes upon her, the woman who had been the last passenger to board on their plane trip was striding confidently towards their booth. She waved her hand at Rosie, who stood up immediately and trotted over to intercept the woman. Rosie made an elaborate show of embracing the woman, kissing the air either side of her cheek but not actually touching. She drew the woman close to where Satine and Ava sat and patted the woman's arm as she spoke:

'Satine. Ava. Allow me to introduce Cicely. Your Mixed Emotions sister!'

Cicely looked down at the two women with an amused indifference at first, but after a few seconds she seemed to decide that she was comfortable and smiled. Unlike Rosie, Satine noted, Cicely's eyes seemed to engage when she smiled.

'You were on our plane.' Ava articulated the thought for both of them.

'Was I?' Cicely slid into the booth beside them and they were both struck by the subtle and intoxicating aroma of her perfume. 'My taxi was late and I only just made the flight. I must have been very flustered – I didn't notice anyone or anything.'

Both Satine and Ava had a mental flashback image of Cicely as she had boarded the plane. The image was of an individual for whom being 'flustered' seemed impossible. This sensation of an untruth being told belied the apparent warmth and disarming words Cicely had chosen.

'So…Cicely,' Ava said after a few moment, 'where are you staying?'

'Oh, I have friends here. I stay with them.' Cicely spoke in the same warm, friendly manner but it was clear that she was not going to elaborate any further. Satine, not willing to let Rosie think that anything was settled concerning the conversation about their expected 'work', took the opportunity to steer the focus back to the topic they had been on before the arrival of Cicely.

'And are you going to be working here too?'

'Ah,' Cicely chuckled softy. 'Rosie has been telling you about the work. I have been doing it for the last month. It's fun, really! No problems!'

Of course, thought Satine: the arrival of Cicely had been perfectly and deliberately timed by Rosie. The work was outlined by Rosie and then Cicely would be on hand to reassure them that it was safe. Before she could continue, Ava had a question of her own for Cicely:

'But you were on our plane! You've only just arrived, surely.'

'No, I had just gone back to England for a few days. Really,' she looked from Satine to Ava and then let her eyes drift over to Rosie. 'I know you have questions, but it is all okay. Is this your first time in Germany?'

'First time anywhere for me. It's all a bit -' Satine's eyes flashed across to the screen on the wall that was now, mercifully, just a blank square of white light. 'Well, it's all a bit overwhelming.' Cicely nodded and, in a move that was as curiously welcome as it was unexpected, she rested her hand on Satine's wrist.

'I know. But try to relax. It will be fine, you'll see.' Satine found herself gazing into Cicely's eyes. There was certainly something mysterious, unknowable about the woman. However, there was also something that struck Satine as heartfelt in her words now and in the touch of her hand. After a few moments, Cicely removed her hand and promptly excused herself, saying that she would see them both soon. She nodded to Rosie as she departed, a gesture that Satine thought denoted approval of herself and Ava.

Rosie disappeared for a few minutes and they could hear her barking instructions from behind the bar area. Satine was surprised to see the cute, Adam Faith lookalike appear behind the bar and start tidying up. Seeming to sense her gaze, he looked across and flashed Satine a sweet little grin. She smiled back, her spirits uplifted considerably just by the sight of him. Ava nudged her, smiling in understanding of Satine's palpable upturn of mood.

'Cute.'

Satine did not need to comment. 'Cute' said it all.

Rosie re-appeared at that point, informing Ava and Satine that Weiler would be taking them back to the apartment. They would have the rest of the day to themselves but be brought back to the Kasbah that evening. Although her heart sank at the thought of what the night would bring, she was momentarily uplifted once more by the sight of Mr Cute who was now in the lounge area, wiping tables. As they followed Rosie toward chrome staircase that led to the reception and exit, they passed right by him.

'Getting to be a habit seeing you,' Ava said as they passed him, knowing that his eyes were on Satine.

'Lukas,' he announced, smiling briefly at Ava but then looking directly back at Satine.

'Well, Lukas,' Ava replied, 'I'm Ava. This is Satine.'

'Nice to –' before Lukas could continue, Rosie rasped from the foot of the stairs that Weiler had arrived and they would have to go. Lukas shrugged and returned to his wiping, giving Satine a final sweet grin.

The afternoon seemed to race away from Satine as she felt the horrible knot of dread tighten in her stomach for the return to Klub Kasbah. Ava seemed less perturbed, although she had disappeared for one of her endless baths which was a sign that all was not well in her state of mind either. Conscious of wanting to sound as upbeat as possible, Satine decided that she would make her first call home that afternoon. So far, she could put a brave face on her experiences and maintain the upbeat tone that she knew her mother would need her to adopt. Tomorrow, thought Satine, and it might be more difficult to put up a brave front. She waited for her call to be connected after painstakingly dialling the international code. The telephone seemed to ring for an age and she was beginning to think that her mother was not home. Then, just as Satine was about to hang up, her mother's voice sounded in her ear. Even the simple word of 'hello' was enough for Satine to find that she was immediately stifling a sob. The distinct Jamaican accent sounded like honey in Satine's ear and she had to fight to compose herself. Before she could reply, Iodine Simone said:

'Satine? Is that my baby girl?' The rich, elongated trill of the vowel sounds was like a soothing balm and Satine felt a tear begin to snake down her cheek.

'Hello, Momma.' She could barely raise her voice above a whisper, fearful that a sob would burst from her throat.

'Ah, baby girl,' Iodine's voice purred. ' How are you, darling? Have you eaten right? What sort of a place have they found for you? Is it clean? Is it a nice area?' The bombardment of questions found Satine having to drop the receiver to her lap for a moment. She shook herself reproachfully and then put the receiver back to her face.

'I'm fine, momma. The place is really nice. Really clean.' She had lost the thread of the questions at this point but rapidly remembered exactly what her mother's priorities would be regardless of where Satine had travelled to or with whom she was currently surrounded. Was it clean? Are you eating right? Are the people good and decent (ideally, Christians)? Nothing ever changed. The same questions would be rolled out as a matter of course if Satine had travelled to the corner shop as a child or whenever work took her off to a new town.

'I said, child, are you eatin' well? Are the people decent?' Satine smiled at the dropped 'g' on 'eating' as it was one of the few lapses of grammar that Iodine allowed to infiltrate her speech. She prided herself on speaking correctly, never swearing and or using 'ugly talk' as she would call it. The obsession with eating well came from an innate confidence that the only food worth eating was the admittedly sumptuous Jamaican fayre that Iodine had been taught by her own mother, who in turn had been taught by her mother. Growing up, Satine has reached a level of competence at making the hearty meals that Iodine had lovingly prepared. As a dancer, she knew that she could burn off a lot of the carbohydrate heavy dishes that were the staple of her mother's recipes. However, Iodine's food always called for every gas burner to be fully ablaze for hours and every pot and pan called into service. Replicating such food in a tiny bedsit was impossible. Plus, Iodine's portions seemed to start with making enough food for a minimum of ten people. Someone leaving Iodine's table capable of walking more than a few yards before collapsing into a stupor of blissfully satiated slumber was unforgivable.

'I'm eating really well. They cooked breakfast for us this morning before our audition!' This was true, at least. 'Everyone has been really nice. Friendly. Helpful.' This not quite as true. Satine found an image of Weiler's scowling face pop into her mind like a spectre, but chased it away with the cute smile of Lukas.

'What are your costumes like? Do you need me to start on anything yet?' The next topic after food and the 'decency' of those around Satine was always the question of whether Iodine should take the covers off her sewing machine. Since the earliest school pageants and nativity plays, Satine was always kitted out in costumes that would have graced a West End production. Iodine's flair and attention to detail meant that Satine had always stood out, even in minor roles. It had been this which had fuelled her love of performing, and the larger roles came in line with the ambitious costumes, as Iodine knew they would. Iodine's own ambitions on stage were confined to the gospel choir performances at church. And 'performance' was the key word as her voice would soar above all others, becoming louder as her excitement grew until her own pipes were in danger of overwhelming those of the church organ.

'No, momma, no costumes mentioned yet. We only just did the sound audition.' Not a complete lie, thought Satine.

'So what are you doing with your time now?' Trust Iodine to zone in on the big question. The honest answer would seem that Satine and Ava were about to become hustling escorts at best in the grim environs of Klub Kasbah. Satine found the image of the porn film on the wall flash into her mind and she imagined her mother's disgust and outrage. She could see her mother dragging Satine and Ava out of the place by their ears whilst denouncing everyone else in the club as 'worse than the devil himself.' Although Iodine's categories of what was good and what was bad were alarmingly unambiguous, Satine found that she almost missed the moral certainty of her mother's world. She had long been used to editing the details of the work she had taken on since leaving home so as not to outrage Iodine, but today's events had been new territory even for someone recently liberated from a chorus line of naked Romans!

'A lot of promotion work at the moment, they say. We met another band member today. She seems nice.' Satine heard her own words and had to admit that she was not sure that the evaluation of Cicely was truthful either. But, for now and for her mother's ears, 'nice' would do. Conscious and a little relieved that a few minutes had ticked by, Satine added: 'Listen, momma, I will have to go. They let us use the telephone here in our apartment as long as we don't stay on for long. It's expensive.'

'I know, baby girl. You go on, now.' Iodine's voice was brittle, taking on that falsely hardened tone of a mother who was having to use tough love when forcing a child to the dentist or into school to face someone who had been mean to them in the playground. Satine knew her mother was getting emotional.

'I will call you next Sunday, momma. After you've got back from church, okay?'

'Okay, baby. I love you.'

The sound of the last three words almost broke Satine at that point. She managed a breathless reply of 'I love you too, momma' and replaced the receiver. She slid down the wall into a foetal heap on the floor and sobbed uncontrollably. Ava heard her cries from the bathroom and, hastily wrapping herself in towels, was soon holding Satine tightly, stroking and comforting her friend. Without fully realising it, Ava was sobbing too.

Weiler arrived at the door of the apartment at six o'clock that evening, carrying two elegant, sheer cocktail dresses in protective covers. He told them that Rosie had selected the dresses for them to wear that evening and she had opted for black for both of them as they would surely have shoes that would match easily. Neither Satine or Ava cared for the dresses, finding the sequined look rather tacky, but they were at least grateful that the cut of the gowns was not too high at the bottom even if the neckline was very plunging.

They had expected worse, based on what they had seen of the club that morning.

Weiler, as taciturn as ever, drove them to the club in time for their rendezvous with Rosie at nine o'clock. Approaching the venue at night, Satine and Ava were pleasantly surprised by the nocturnal transformation. A neon sign proclaiming 'Klub Kasbah' with an accompanying fez and exclamation mark revolved on a pole at the top of the building. The doorway, bland in the daylight, had taken on a much more inviting aspect now that the hundred or so bulbs around the heavy swing doors were shining. A velvet rope barrier snaked along the nearside of the pavement and two huge men in tuxedos stood like sentinels either side of the doorway. The presence of the bouncers was reassuring for Satine and Ava. There would evidently be plenty of muscle if any of the customers crossed the line. Weiler walked them to the doors, exchanging a few words with the security men and then sauntered off to his Mercedes, saying that Rosie would arrange a taxi for them later that evening and for them to 'not make any noise' when they returned. Ava's extended middle finger, jabbed aggressively upwards in the direction of Weiler's back summed up both women's reactions in a more than eloquent manner. One of the bouncers gave a reassuring chuckle as he noticed Ava's gesture.

The reception area was still fairly quiet, but when they arrived a small clutch of people were standing in a circle around an animated Rosie. She looked glamorous in a long black dress with a white sash; her short hair was slicked back to evoke a thirties look which suited her well. When she spotted Satine and Ava, she broke away from the circle and made her way over to them. She looked them up and down and nodded with self-approval at her choice of attire for them.

'Girls! You look charming. Come!' With that, she turned on her heels and made her way to the staircase. Even the staircase looked better than before, with the chrome fittings shining under a network of fairy lights and the tears in the carpet blending into the darkness. The main bar area and dance floor was equally transformed. The stale odours had been replaced with a mixture of tobacco smoke and perfume, mixed with the tang of the dry ice that periodically blasted a cloud onto the dance floor. The music was a pulsating beat of disco sounds, seeming even louder because there were only about twenty people in the club at this point. They followed Rosie to the same booth where they had sat earlier in the day. Now, the scratched table top looked smooth under the soft patina from an ornate lamp in its centre. Overhead spotlights with red bulbs cast a warm glow on the velvet booth, masking the stains and rips. Overall, the club was like Cinderella's coach before midnight: if you looked closely, the mice and the pumpkin could still be detected - but nobody was looking that closely. Not that Prince Charming's palace went in for pornography on the walls – not even in the darkest of the versions conjured up by the brothers Grimm! Satine and Ava tried their best to ignore the lurid display which was, at least, only pictures this time as the music obliterated the grunting and groaning of the soundtrack. Sliding into the booth, Ava and Satine positioned themselves so that they were facing away from projection screen. They noticed that the podiums by the dance floor were also empty. However, with few customers at this stage in the evening it seemed likely that this would change when there was more of an audience.

'We have two lovely gentlemen visiting the club tonight. Both from England! So, that will be nice for you! Big potential investors in Mixed Emotions, so please be charm personified!' Rosie shouted above the din of the music. At this, she stalked off towards the bar and began shouting orders at the small group of bar staff. With regret, Satine noticed that Lukas was not amongst them. Reading her frown, Ava said:

'Maybe it's his night off. Or he might be starting later. It's hardly busy at the moment.'

'True,' Satine smiled at Ava. Tonight would be tough, but nowhere near as testing as it would be if they did not have each other. The two sat in silence for a time, gazing around the room as customers began to appear at the top of the stairs and fill up the booths. There were some couples, but mostly the customers were small groups of men. Each time a group of two appeared, Satine and Ava scrutinised them in anticipation that these would be their 'companions' for the evening. However, each booth was almost full before Rosie returned to them to say that the two 'lovely gentlemen' were running late but would be with them soon.

Shortly after Rosie disappeared again, the lights dimmed and two harsh spotlights were switched on above the dancing podiums. Unobserved by Satine and Ava, two women had taken up position on the platforms. One, a tall Barbadian woman with a slightly Arabic look and a mane of naturally wavy hair fashioned in a long ponytail was starting to sway to the music. She had a beautiful, curvy figure, most of which was on display save for a skimpy gold bikini. She wore impossibly high strappy shoes in matching gold. Nevertheless, even with heels and her natural height, the woman was dwarfed by the woman who occupied the podium to her left: it was as if a Valkyrie had fallen off a winged chariot en route to Valhalla and landed in a strip club. In a matching ensemble to her companion, the woman looked to be nearly seven feet tall. Her short, white-blonde hair stood up like a halo around her beautifully blue eyes. Her skin was pale and flawless, her legs seemingly endless. She seemed to be wearing little if any make-up, but there was a glowing translucence about her skin that made her look like an alabaster statue of a goddess. The two began to writhe to the music in a way that was captivating, even for Satine and Ava. A hush fell over the room as the collected groups of men became fixated on every swish of the ponytail, every sway of hips. The taller woman seemed to radiate confidence in her performance, smiling throughout. Her companion looked much more distant, as if she had learned to take her mind elsewhere. The dance lasted about five minutes, with men approaching the podiums in increasing numbers, depositing bank notes at the feet of the women in exchange for being blown kisses. By the end of the performance, both women had removed their bikini tops, which increased the flurry of activity to throw more money onto the podiums. The Valkyrie finished her dance by removing the entirety of her outfit save for the shoes. The other woman refrained from this final remove. As confident as anyone could be, the blonde giant stalked off and through a door by the D.J.s booth, swinging her discarded bikini in her left hand as she walked. The other woman hastily put her bikini top back on before following, in an incongruous display of modesty that made Satine wince. Both women noticed that neither dancer had collected any of the banknotes that practically filled the surface area of the podiums. As they watched, Rosie scurried over to the podiums and gathered them up, disappearing off through the same door that the dancers had just exited through.

'I wonder how much of that cash they get?' Ava mused.

'Mm,' replied Satine, 'something tells me not as much as Rosie!'

The lights had raised again slightly after the podium show had concluded. As her eyes adjusted to the change, Satine noticed that Cicely had arrived at the club. Dressed in an identical cocktail number (did Rosie have a deal with a clothing factory?), Cicely was flanked by two balding,

sweaty little men in creased suits. They followed her to a
vacant booth, one listing drunkenly as he lurched in her
wake. The other, dazed by alcohol but more sturdy on his
feet, was carrying a large silver ice bucket. From the top of
the bucket, Satine could see to neck of a bottle of
champagne. In his free hand, a bunch of fluted glasses
were perched by their stems between his fat, hairy fingers.
Rosie stood at the bar, nodding knowingly to Cicely as the
men slid awkwardly into the booth. Too far away for their
voices to be heard above the din of the music, Satine and
Ava became transfixed by the performance that unfolded
like a silent movie before them. Cicely seemed to find
every word the two men said to be a nugget of comedy
genius, tipping her head back in peels of laughter and
patting the men on their hands whenever they spoke. One
of the men, the lurcher, attempted to place a cigarette
between his wet lips. He failed in this endeavour, the
cigarette dropping into his lap. In a flash, Cicely plucked it
up and placed it to his lips. She produced a lighter, igniting
the cigarette for the man. He smiled in appreciation, the
cigarette nearly falling out of his mouth and back into his
lap. The champagne carrier started to fill the three flutes,
his hand steadier than his companions but still jerky. As
Satine and Ava watched, Cicely slid her palm across the

table so that the tips of her fingers rested against the base of one of the flutes. The man filled each glass in turn, topping them up when the foaming bubbles had diminished. The entire bottle was soon emptied, a good proportion of its contents having fizzled away into the air. The man moved to place the now empty bottle on the table. It was at that precise moment that Cicely pushed out with her finger tips, toppling the nearest glass into its companions. Two of the glasses fell onto their sides, the other falling off the table completely. The timing was immaculate, as the 'accident' happened at the moment the empty bottle was placed on the table, thereby making it seem that the man had somehow caught one of the flutes as his arm descended. Cicely was on her feet immediately, expertly faking shock and darting out of the way of the slick of champagne that coated the table and started to drip over the sides. The two men, laps now expensively sodden, began scrabbling to avoid the dripping edges of the table. The smoking man turned on the other, angrily thumping him on the arm for his apparent clumsiness. As Satine and Ava watched with increasing amusement and admiration, Cicely fussed around the two men, wiping their laps and then the table with the heavy napkin that had been wrapped around the neck of the bottle. Moments later, Rosie appeared with three fresh flutes and another bottle. The men waved their acquiescence to the fresh purchase and, this time, Cicely poured the champagne.

'My God! She's brilliant!' Ava gasped in amazement. Satine had to agree. Moments later, Rosie was at their table. She leaned over to them and smiled:

'I think you have just had a masterclass, girls -no? Just in time too – your companions for this evening have just arrived.'

She gestured over to a pair of similarly creased and drunken-looking men who had appeared at the top of the staircase. Rosie trotted over to them, herding them to the bar.

Moments later, the two men were at the table – one holding an ice bucket with champagne, the other clutching four champagne flutes…

Later, after a taxi ride home and a warm shower, Satine sat on the edge of Ava's bed as they recounted the night's events. The temptation to roar with laughter was constant, but each attempted to subdue the other for fear of incurring the wrath of Weiler as it was, by then, 4am. The two British drunks had actually been harmless and quite sweet.

One had been a little over-familiar and his hands wandered to Satine's knee at one point, but he had been quickly reprimanded by his companion. They were both from Birmingham, in Hanover to view a new piece of machinery that they were thinking of buying for their canning factory. The two men had talked enthusiastically and endlessly about both the machine and their business. Who knew that dog food canning processes could be so intricate and fascinating? Both women had felt a little guilty until the men produced a catalogue of the latest canning component innovations. After that, sympathy went out of the window. And, strangely, first one of the men and then the other found that they grew exceedingly clumsy as the night wore on, both spilling a full bottle of champagne! It was just as well that Rosie, ever the attentive hostess, was on hand to replace the bottles with fresh ones.

They were still on the nursery slopes compared to the queen of this particular scam, but before too long they would be able to give Cicely a run for their money.

It was not as if they would not get plenty of time to perfect their routine.

Chapter Four – The Ball Starts to Roll…?

The days and nights blended into quite a seamless routine after the first two weeks in Hanover. Satine and Ava were taken to Klub Kasbah every other night, each time spending a few hours in the company of a couple of alarmingly clumsy men. Their days were spent sleeping late and hanging around the apartment. Rosie had spent the first week telling them that work on Mixed Emotions would soon begin in earnest.

However, by the second week this no longer featured in her conversation. Satine and Ava resolved that they would keep quiet until the start of week three. They both wanted to talk with Cicely, but it seemed that after that first night, they were taken to the club at times when Cicely was not there. Rosie had explained that Cicely was working on the nights that the women were not at the club and that they would have time to get to know each other soon enough. Ava shrugged this off, but Satine could not help but think that Rosie was keeping them apart deliberately. Divide and conquer was a phrase that came to mind. As the days went by, the reasons to dislike Rosie mounted up. She still maintained the false air of friendliness, but it was clear that she was bored now with the effort of trying particularly hard. She still came by the apartment frequently, often with bags of groceries or some money for them to 'enjoy Hanover with' but her visits were fleeting, and it was clear that they were perfunctory and designed to keep them sweet. Nor had there been any sign or mention of S.K. since their time at the recording studio. Whenever Satine or Ava tried to bring up his name, Rosie shot it down with a phrase such as 'Oh, such a busy guy!' or 'I am music industry widow!'

Regular nights at the club meant that the two women had started to get to know some of the other workers. Lukas worked behind the bar some evenings, it seemed but was mostly employed during the daytime to clean and stock up. It turned out that he was a musician and sound recordist, kept busy at the club like the others until the 'real work' started. Satine hoped to see him each night they went to the club, but she had been disappointed since the first day. They had also got to know one of the two dancers who they had watched on their first night. The impossibly tall Valkeyrie turned out to have (or at least use) the glorious name of Lotte Love. She was as intelligent as she was beautiful, speaking four languages fluently in addition to her native Danish. Satine and Lotte hit it off straight away, often chatting at the end of the evening as they waiting for their taxis. Seemingly unaware of her beauty and cleverness, Lotte had absolutely no edge to her at all. She approached everybody with warmth and it was clear that everyone had a good word for her at the club. Satine asked her why she wasn't working as a translator at the Hague and earning a fortune, but Lotte had just laughed and said that, for the moment at least, what she was doing was 'more fun.' Lotte's parents were both university lecturers and she came from an extremely cultured and conservative background. They had no idea that she was stripping in Hanover, of course, but Lotte really didn't seem to care one way or the other if they ever found out. She was, as she told Satine, 'Enjoying the freedom while it lasted' and there seemed an acceptance that, at some point soon, the Hague would come calling or something equally worthy and that would be the end of the wild Lotte Love.

After a particularly dull evening, Satine sat with Lotte at the foot of the staircase. Ava had gone home early, complaining of a headache. Weiler had picked her up, actually being quite concerned and charming. Satine, convinced that he would not have been anywhere near as sympathetic if it had been her that had taken ill had aired her thoughts to Lotte.

'Mm,' Lotte paused in her usual manner as they waited for exactly the right words to come to her before she spoke. 'Weiler is a curious man. Not as tough as he might seem, I think.'

'I thought it was my colour he didn't like at first, until I saw the 'lost love' on the wall.'

'Ah, yes. The famous Danka.' Lotte smiled and looked at Satine, reading her reaction to the name. Seeing that there was none, Lotte continued thoughtfully: 'She is the lost love, indeed. Apparently, he has never got over her. He keeps that picture in the guest apartment but can't stand to have it in his own, you know?'

'Odd?'

'Maybe. Maybe not. I think he needs to know that he can look at it from time to time, but only on his terms. He couldn't bear to see it every day.' Lotte's observations had such an empathic logic to them that Satine knew instinctively that Lotte had evaluated the situation perfectly.

'So, you think he is prickly because his heart is still broken?' Satine found herself wanting to be the bigger person but could still not get past the dislike that Weiler had instilled.

'That…and other things. I think he has had to endure more than any of us can imagine – losing Danka the most painful part of it. I think that, perhaps, you might remind him a little of her.'

Satine nodded slowly. Could this explain Weiler's hostility? The reason why he found it easier to be nicer to Ava? Satine saw that Lotte was looking directly at her, like a patient teacher who knew that their student was on the brink of figuring out the answer to a question. She began to realise that she had picked up on only half of what Lotte had said.

'What 'other things'?'

'It is no secret, so I will say it. But,' Lotte gave Satine a very straight look, 'I think you will wait until he tells you himself before you say I said it? Weiler is transgender.'

Lotte allowed Satine time to process this information. It suddenly seemed quite obvious, and Satine felt a mixture of foolishness and shame. Katrinka Weiler. He has kept his birth name. Satine knew little of the process for gender re-assignment, as in the UK it was still a topic that was not spoken about or treated with compassion. She knew that, even though homosexuality had been de-criminalised nearly a decade earlier, the reality for gay men was difficult enough. She had met many young men in chorus lines who lived in fear of their families finding out about their true identity, embracing the sanctuary and anonymity of London but still forced to live a life of looking over their shoulders and never knowing if a landlord would kick them out or an employer show them the door. Satine lived with prejudice every day, but she knew that there were places where she could escape it. What sanctuary was there for someone like Weiler? His hard exterior made a lot of sense now. How else would he survive?

'Wow.' Satine said at length. 'I guess I just didn't think of that. It is still a taboo subject back home.'

'Better here, to some extent. Still difficult. Things are better back home, strangely enough.' Lotte chuckled at the reality of her native country. She might be overseas to break out of her conservative family constraints, but the truth was that she was from one of the most liberal and forward-thinking of countries. 'Weiler was able to…become himself in Denmark. That makes me proud.'

'Yes,' Satine nodded, 'I can see that. You know, Rosie said something when we first met her that makes sense now. She called him Frau Weiler. A slip of the tongue?'

'No,' Lotte concluded with sage wisdom, 'it was not a slip of the tongue. Rosie said that because she is a cunt.'

'The Hague does not know what it's missing!' Satine laughed. As if on cue, Rosie appeared to announce that their taxis had arrived. Satine was not sure whether or not Rosie's sour expression was owing to the fact that it had been a long night or whether she had actually heard Lotte's apt evaluation. She really hoped that it was the latter.

As she climbed out of the taxi, Satine noticed that the lounge light was still on in Weiler's. As she made her way into the building, she hesitated by the door to Weiler's apartment. She knocked softly on the door. For a moment, there was silence, but just as she was turning to ascend the stairs, the door opened slightly. Weiler, wrapped in a crimson dressing gown and holding a tumbler of bandy, peered out at her with defensive curiosity.

'Problem?' The default hostility was evident.

'No….sorry, Mr Weiler. I saw your light was on. I just wanted to say…' Satine found her words dried in her throat. She became aware of the soft sound of classical music coming from the gap in the door. Bach.

'To say…?' Weiler stared at her as if she was mad or drunk. Or both.

'I wanted to say, 'Satine found her words at last: 'I wanted to say thank you. Thank you for looking after us. I realised, I guess, that…that I haven't said that to you.'

Feeling very foolish, Satine could only blink at Weiler as he continued to stare at her like she was an exhibit in a Victorian freak show. Then, after an endless moment, he nodded.

'You are welcome. Now, goodnight.'

With that he closed the door in Satine's face. However, Satine thought as she climbed the stairs, he had not slammed the door and she could swear that the corners of his mouth had formed into a little smile as it closed.

The following day brought with it the miracle: Rosie appeared in the early afternoon and informed them that there would be a photo shoot the following morning in Klub Kasbah for all four members of Mixed Emotions. Such was their excitement that neither Ava or Satine thought to question the mathematics of the statement until after Rosie has breezed out of the apartment.

'She said four.' The thought occurred to Ava as she was making coffee.

'Yeah, she did.' Satine frowned. 'I wonder who the other girl is, then.'

'Lotte? That would be a blast!'

'No. Lotte would have said. Besides, I don't think she can sing.'

'They don't actually know or seem to care whether I can!' Ava reminded.

The rest of the day was spent in speculation, but they heard nothing else from Rosie. In the early evening, they heard Weiler arrive back home. He knocked on their door and presented them with two large boxes. Inside, there were identical costumes for the photo shoot. Both had been given gleaming white rubberised catsuits with electric blue feather boas. Ava had been a given beaded hat that made her look like Betty Boop. Satine had been gifted with a fedora in the same electric blue as the boas. The footwear was heeled silver boots.

'Are they kidding?' Ava groaned.

'I did an episode of Doctor Who last year. Two days in a quarry in Kent playing a non-speaking handmaiden to an alien queen that resembled a giant green penis. The costume they gave me was made out of that stuff they packed China plates in to stop them getting broken. It rained solidly and the costume fell apart so they put me in a fire curtain, tied at the waist with a piece of tinsel, for the last day. The rain stopped and it was snowing instead.' Satine shivered at the memory. 'The girl playing the Doctor's assistant felt so sorry for me that she gave me her gloves.' Satine held the catsuit up to the light. 'It was still miles better than this shit!'

Taking advantage of a night away from the club, Ava and Satine pampered and preened themselves before taking to their beds very early. Dressed in the chosen costumes and feeling like children who had been caught playing dress-up in their mother's bedroom, they climbed into Weiler's car and were driven to the club for their morning shoot. If Weiler found their costumes as ridiculous as they did themselves, he betrayed nothing in his typically taciturn manner. However, Satine did notice that he actually wished her 'good morning' and held the passenger door open for her to slide into the rear seat. Such courtesies, (if they happened at all), were usually reserved for Ava who had, since their arrival, seemed to have been slightly more in favour. Satine was pleased that she had thanked him, feeling that something had thawed a little.

The club was even quieter than it had been on their first morning visit. The only member of staff on duty was Lukas. Satine was initially delighted to see his cute, smiling face as he waved at her from behind the bar. He was perched on a pair of step ladders, busily cleaning some of the higher shelves. She was just admiring the pert, roundness of his bum in the tight, faded jeans he was wearing when the realisation of how she must have appeared to him in her hideous outfit dawned on her in a flash. He seemed like he was about to make his way over to talk to her but, her face burning hot with embarrassment, Satine gave him a quick wave and then turned away and slid into the nearest booth that was facing away from the bar.

'What's up with you?' Ava hissed, sliding next to her. 'I thought you liked him.'

'I do! But in these clothes!' Satine whispered, her face still burning. Moments later, she wished that the ground would open and swallow her as she heard Ava shout across to the bar:

'Satine says it's lovely to see you! She can't talk at the moment, Lukas, but she will catch up with you after we do the photo shoot.'

'No problem! Lovely to see you both!' Lukas shouted back. Satine looked over to the sound of his voice, forgiving Ava instantly and feeling grateful. She smiled at Lukas and waved again. He smiled back, his broad grin emphasising the dimples in his cheeks.

'By the way, Lukas – nice bum!' shouted Ava, reducing Satine back into a state of mortification. In response to this, Lukas climbed back up the step ladders and gave them a wiggle of the bum in question. First Ava and then Satine roared with laughter.

'Glad to see you in great spirits, girls!'

The sound of Rosie's shrill tones ended their mirth in an instant. She stood at the top of the staircase, her hair hidden by a powder blue turban and wearing a matching jump suit and silver heels. At her side stood a young man, probably about twenty years old but with a boyishness about him that meant he could have passed for a Sixth

Form student. He had curly black hair that framed his pale face like a Roman statue, his eyes dark brown and fringed with impossibly long lashes. His lips were sensual, like Mick Jagger's and his body was lithe and athletic. Both women could take in the unmarked, youthful beauty of the man quite clearly, as aside from a feather boa in the same hue as Satine's, he wore only a skimpy pair of silver shorts and matching thigh boots.

'Ladies! This is Claude.' Rosie walked the young man over to them, and they jumped to their feet to shake his hand. He smiled readily, betraying a little shyness and understandable self-consciousness about his outfit. Able to take in their costumes as they stood up, Claude seemed to relax a little. He looked no more ridiculous that they did and there was always safety in numbers.

'And Cicely makes four!' Rosie trilled, and all of them looked back to the staircase where Cicely had just emerged. There was no time or opportunity to confer, but Satine, Ava and Claude all experienced the same thought when they looked at Cicely: she was dressed in silver with a blue boa and a sparkly Betty Boop mesh hat, very much in keeping with the overall look. However, her actual dress was a flowing and elegant gown with a matching cape. The neckline was plunging, the dress slit high to show her shapely legs to full effect. There was, to the annoyance of the others, something more elegant and sophisticated about her overall look. It was obviously more expensive and something that Ava and Satine would have felt quite comfortable wearing. The billowing fabrics made Claude feel even more aware of his naked torso. Above all, the costume made Cicely look like the star. Instantly, the others felt that they had been cast as anonymous Ikettes to Cicely as Tina. Rosie seemed unconcerned by the disparity between the outfits, but Cicely showed some reassuring discomfort as she took in the costumes that Ava, Satine and Claude were wearing.

'How do you like the look? I was a bit surprised myself!' Cicely said quickly and diplomatically. Satine interpreted the words correctly and smiled. The costumes were meant to cause division, that was clear. But the responsibility for this would seem to be nothing to do with Cicely. She could have been deliberately trying to shift blame, of course, but there was something about her embarrassment when she saw them that told Satine that Cicely was not lying. She shot Rosie a look, remembering Lotte's appraisal of her and finding no reason to question it.

'Sooo' Rosie flittered across to the dance floor, carefully avoiding making eye contact with any of them. 'The photographer will be here with S.K. in a little while. You will take the pictures here. Mixed Emotions begins this day!' She threw her arms wide in a dramatic gesture and tittered unconvincingly.

About half an hour later, S.K. arrived, flanked by a man carrying a complicated, professional camera and a slight, short little man who was carrying a huge box. The box turned out to be full of make-up equipment. Much to their horror, all three of the Mixed Emotions women were set upon by the Rumpelstiltskin figure who first scraped away their perfectly good make-up and then assaulted their faces with thick foundation and garish shades of lipstick and eye-shadow. Even Claude did not escape as first his face and then his torso was coated in foundation and glitter.

After the seemingly endless ordeal, the homunculus scurried off with his box of horrors and the photographer started to bark instructions at them as they took various poses on the dance floor. S.K. stood some way off, watching for the most part but occasionally giving orders to Rosie, who skittered back and forth to the photographer to relay the orders. For the most part, they were arranged in a tight group scenario, with Claude often lying on the floor in the foreground. At all times, Cicely was placed centrally, usually with Satine and Ava flanking her. Each arrangement seemed to emphasise the fact that Cicely was seen as the lead singer.

By early afternoon, the session came to a close. Without much opportunity to exchange more than pleasantries with either Cicely or Claude, Satine and Ava were taken back to the apartment by Weiler. At no point did S.K. engage them directly in conversation, merely growling 'gut!' as a signal that the session was over as he waved a brisk goodbye to them. Rosie assured them that he was delighted and that the shots would look great. Unconvinced, they rested that afternoon after purging themselves of the thick and lurid make-up and prepared for another night at the club.

Two days later, Rosie arrived at the apartment with a folder containing about twenty glossy photographs from the shoot. Mercifully, the make-up did not look as bad on film and even the costumes started to make some kind of sense. There was a cohesive look to the group and the group shots would not have been out of place on the cover of an album. The photographer had made the background of the club hazy and applied some sort of trickery that made them look like they were standing in outer space. The central positioning of Cicely in all the shots was, if anything, even more obvious in the photographs than it had been in the club. After Rosie had left, Ava turned to Satine and said:

'You know, we could be cropped out of most of those pictures, and nobody would even know we were meant to be there.'

'True,' Satine frowned. 'But you could say the same for Claude. He was on the floor for most of the time. Cut those pictures off at waist height and we become the racially mixed Three Degrees!'

'He seemed nice.'

'Mm.' Satine looked at Ava with curiosity. 'How...nice?'

'Oh, please!' Ava laughed. 'He wouldn't be interested in me! Or you!'

'No,' Satine concurred, 'definitely not. I saw him looking at Lukas a few times. Seems we aren't the only ones to appreciate a nice bum when we see one!'

'So, what's next I wonder.'

'An actual recording session? Would that be too much to expect?'

For the next two weeks, it seemed that it was indeed too much to expect. The women spent their now usual routine of nights on and nights off at the club, perfecting their carelessness with expensive drinks and feeling increasingly alienated from the dreams that had brought them to Hanover in the first place.

There were changes on the horizon – but not anything like they would have imagined.

Chapter Five – Some Enchanted Evening.

The chill of the Hanover night air made the man wince as he stepped out of the airport arrivals section of the building. He scanned the street before him, locating the nearest phone box and sprinting towards it. Grateful for the temporary sanctuary, he pulled the concertina door across behind him and fed the payphone with coins. The familiar whirs and clicks filled his ears as he waited for the call to connect. Eventually, he heard the familiar flat tone of his boss:

'Dakin.'

'Boss, it's Cooper. I've arrived.' The man shivered despite the shielding of the booth as the wind whipped around the airport building and rattled the folding door. 'You were right about the cold here. It's even worse than London-'

'Never mind the pissing weather report!' Dakin's voice snapped. 'Check into the hotel and then get yourself off to the club. You have the address?'

'Yep,' Cooper replied, angry at himself for expecting Dakin to be any less the officious martinet than he had been when they had first met in London. The man had no charm in person, much less a telephone manner. 'Klub Kasbah.'

'You've got your cover story by heart, I hope.'

'Yes, sir.'

'See that you have! And remember,' growled Dakin, 'don't make direct contact with her unless I say so. She's no fool.' With that, Dakin disconnected the phone. Cooper frowned, collecting the unspent coins that dropped in to the little tray below the receiver as the call ended. Dakin was bloody miserable – even for a Pom! He turned up his collar and placed the coins into a little side pouch in his wallet. As he did so, he noticed the corner of a small photograph had started to edge its way out of the wallet. He plucked the picture out, taking a moment to look at it even though he knew the image so well.

Cicely looked back up at him from the photograph.

Moments later, Cooper scurried out of the phone booth as the rain began to fall, darting into a vacant taxi.

The club was very quiet that evening, and Rosie had decreed that there would be no strip show. This meant that Lotte and her fellow dancer, Tamara, were allowed to take off early. Both had decided to take Rosie up on a rare offer of a free drink and sat with Satine and Ava. The latter had not had any drinks to spill that night thus far and were enjoying the company of the two women. Lotte was her usual bubbly and flamboyant self, mercilessly ripping into Rosie as she watched her berate the bar staff for no apparent reason. Tamara was a very different type of personality and both Ava and Satine were shocked by the timidity that seemed to be her defining feature. Her refined looks too were more elegant than glamorous and it seemed that an art gallery or theatre front of house would be a more fitting location for Tamara. There was a sadness in her eyes, Satine noted, a sense that her mind was frequently elsewhere and her preoccupation meant that she often seemed to drift away from them in mid-conversation.

'How long have you been in Hanover?' Ava ventured, noting Tamara's obviously British accent.

'Nine months and five days.' Tamara replied as if she was a prisoner who had been etching a line for each day on the wall of her cell. 'But I hope to go home for a week next month.' Tamara smiled at this, her thoughts clearly taking her to a prospect that was keenly anticipated.

'And where is home exactly? I'm guessing Kent maybe?' Satine asked.

'Brighton, actually,' Tamara replied. 'My mum has a guest house there.'

'Sounds nice. I love Brighton.'

'Me too. Wish I could stay there.' Tamara's eyes glistened at these words, and Satine felt like she had said the wrong thing by even mentioning the seaside town. Lotte patted Tamara's hand and said:

'Tam misses her babies. They live with her mum.'

'You have children? How many?' Ava asked, guessing correctly that Tamara would rally at a chance to talk about her babies.

'I have three. Bobby, he's eight now. Then, Lucy, she's six. Molly is four.'

Although her face lit up as she recounted the names, both Satine and Ava found their hearts drop when they heard the ages of the children. Separation from them must be hard enough, Satine thought, but they really were just babies.

'Mum is golden, but there is only so much money coming in and that's all seasonal. Nobody wants to go to the seaside in winter. I wish I could be home.'

Lotte patted Tamara's hand again, saying: 'And in a few weeks you will be home with once more for a lovely holiday. And then soon, home for good!' Tamara smiled affectionately at Lotte. Satine and Ava knew only too well that attitudes toward unmarried mothers back home were still dragging them out of the Dark Ages. Brighton had a more bohemian atmosphere and sensibility that many parts of the UK, but even so, Tamara must have encountered hostility and disapproval.

The two women stayed with Satine and Ava for a few minutes more, before taking their leave of the club. It turned out that Rosie did indeed take a cut of the money that was lavished on them as they performed, but it was surprisingly slight and Ava and Satine could see how both women would be able to pile up quite a considerable amount of (untaxed) cash in a relatively short time. For Tamara, it seemed that this was a lifeline. Both Satine and Ava hoped that it would not be something she would have to endure for very long.

The rest of the night was punctuated by a couple of hapless Danish businessmen, saturated with wine from a conference and banquet to celebrate the international success of a new form of chicken wire. Not suspecting how many tedious facets there could be to the manufacture of chicken wire, Satine and Ava were clumsier than ever and the champagne fridge was quite depleted by the time Rosie's bouncers carried the two men off to a taxi.

Knowing that they would not need to 'work' after this, Satine and Ava decided to take advantage of the opportunity to drink rather than spill the full champagne bottle that sat on the table – both Danes passing out shortly after the third bottle had been presented to them. Satine had excused herself for the bathroom halfway through the bottle, leaving Ava to gaze around the sparsely occupied room. Mercifully, the projector had mysteriously been broken several nights before so the walls were free of the usual porn. Nobody knew exactly how a bottle of nail varnish had tipped itself into the mechanism, but apparently, it would take over a week for the contraption to be repaired. The shade was one favoured by Lotte who, of course, knew absolutely *nothing* about how the projector could have ended up in such a state. The fact that it meant that, on busy nights, both she and Tamara would perform extra dances and probably double their wages was purely a serendipitous coincidence. Ava smiled at the thought that Tamara might be able to return to her babies permanently a lot sooner if such an accident were to happen on a regular basis. And it was always a good idea for a lady such as herself to keep a bottle of nail varnish in her purse at all times.

Ava noticed that Satine had emerged from the ladies' room but had been taken aside by Rosie who was talking to her at the bar. Hoping she would return with some news about 'Mixed Emotions', Ava passed her time by continuing to gaze around at the small clumps of people that populated some of the booths. Her eye fell on a lone figure, unusual in itself. He was young, about thirty she would guess. He had a very serious demeanour but there was no denying that he was very attractive in a rugged manner. His jaw was strong, with a neatly clipped moustache above thin, manly lips. His nose had been broken at some point which somehow added to his overall attractiveness. He had an unruly mop of red hair, a cowlick of which kept falling across his left eye. The eyes themselves were bright and watchful.

Ava realised that she had been staring at the man only when he slid out of the booth he was sitting in and made his way over to where she was sitting. Unlike Satine, Ava had the confidence borne of her private education to bypass shyness and she bade the man a confident welcome as he stood before her and spoke:

'Good evening. This might sound like a terrible line, but I'm new in town and I wonder if I could join you.' The man looked pleased with himself. Noticing his athletic build as he walked over to her, Ava could not help but agree that he had no reason not to be confident. Even from just a few words, she could detect the unmistakable accent of an Australian. The rugged swagger made sense.

'Well, you should know I am here with my friend but yes, I suppose you can join us.'

'I noticed. How could I not notice two beautiful women?' He sat down opposite her, and Ava noticed just how bright his eyes were as he looked directly at her and smiled. 'Lucky for me that the most beautiful one was left alone.'

Corny. Bold. But Ava couldn't help but find this man charming. 'Well, I don't know if that sort of line works in Sydney….'

'It's Melbourne, actually, but not a bad guess.' He reached across the table with his left hand. Noting that it had neither a wedding band or the pale mark where one usually resided, Ava took his hand. 'Glen Cooper. Nice to meet you.'

At the bar, Satine noticed the activity at their booth and she frowned. 'I thought we were free for the rest of the night.'

'You are,' Rosie replied, following Satine's gaze. 'That young man isn't anything to do with me. Rather handsome,' she added. Satine suspected that the last words were designed to provoke jealousy. Feeling none, Satine replied:

'Well, I guess I had better stay here a while longer. Three's a crowd, after all.'

'Mm,' Rosie seemed to be considering her response. After a few moments, it seemed that she had reached a decision and she snapped at the nearest barman to pour them both a glass of champagne.

'A happy bunch of people makes for a successful group!' Rosie raised her glass. Satine found herself a little surprised, but was perversely reassured when Rosie added: 'Just make sure that neither you nor Ava get too distracted by anyone – or pregnant!' This was, at least, true to form.

'He only sat down with her a minute ago, Rosie. I wouldn't think she's likely to have conceived yet!'

Rosie actually laughed at this, in a way that actually seemed genuine as opposed to the tittering peels that she unleashed periodically when she had an audience.

'So, what brings you all the way to Germany?'

'Railways.'

'Hell of a long trip, then. Not to mention wet!' Ava laughed.

'Funny. No, I work in railways. Signal technology, to be precise. I'm here for two months to learn about a new system the Germans have developed. So much of Australia is yet to be connected with a decent network. I'm here to learn and then roll out things back home.'

'Sounds…'

'Boring? It is,' Cooper laughed. 'But it pays well. Bloody amazingly well, to be fair.' If Cooper had guessed that this would be the right thing to say, his confirmation came in the form of Ava's already large eyes widening even more.

'Handsome and rich!' Ava toyed with her champagne flute, swishing the contents around the glass in a little circle. 'So what's the catch?'

'That's a cynical attitude.'

'I'm in show business. It comes with the territory.'

'Show business? That sounds glamorous,' Cooper continued to gaze at Ava, seeming to hang on her every word.

'Oh,' Ava thought about falling polystyrene Roman pillars, itchy wigs, and chicken wire moguls. 'You have no idea how glamorous. Elizabeth Taylor couldn't cope with it!'

'Well,' Cooper leaned forward, still looking at her with those intense eyes. 'Tell me all about it.'

By the time the club closed, Ava had spent an hour in the company of the handsome Australian signalman. Although she had stayed at the bar with Rosie until their taxi had arrived, by the time Ava had finished waxing lyrical about Cooper, she was word-perfect on every part of their conversation. Mercifully, Ava had eventually fallen asleep on the sofa and Satine was able to go to her bed, tenderly wrapping a blanket over her sleeping friend before she turned off the lights and left Ava to dream of the apparently wonderful Glen Cooper. As she turned over that night, Satine felt a warm buzz of delight for her friend. Of course, the fact that it now meant she need not worry about

Ava being left out if Lukas and she were to develop anything was not in the forefront of Satine's mind. Well, not at first anyway.

The following morning, Cooper was already waiting by the telephone box outside his hotel when the phone rang. He shut himself into the booth before picking up the receiver. Dakin's voice sounded as flat and blunt as usual and he offered no greeting save to say:

'Glad you are punctual, Cooper. So, what gives?'

'I've made a contact. A good one.' Cooper caught sight of his reflection in the glass of the booth and gave himself a wink. ' Luck was on my side last night.'

'Luck runs out bloody quickly!' Dakin's voice barked back at him. 'What contact?'

'A Brit. Working for the Shultz-Kloppers too.'

'Well, that's hardly a fucking shock! They run the club.'

'No, but,' Cooper exhaled sharply. He allowed himself the momentary fantasy of what it would feel like to punch Dakin in the face and watch his nose spray blood everywhere. 'She isn't just turning whatever tricks Shultz-Klopper operates in that shithole. He's setting up a pop group, with my contact and the lady in question as part of it.'

'He's done that before, apparently.' Dakin was a hard sell. 'Session singers and one-hit wonder act. It might not mean anything.'

'No, this time it seems Shultz-Klopper wants to take it further. A proper pop group. My contact and her friend were hired by someone called Mueller in London, the same as the suspect.'

'That might explain why she went back and forth to Hanover in the last few months. But keep your distance from her – you hear me? She's sharp.' Dakin sounded even more bitter than usual. Cooper knew that Cicely Walker had been detained by Dakin as she flew out to Hanover for the second time in consecutive months. He also knew that Dakin had got nowhere with her and had to let her take her flight. Dakin's reputation was known throughout Interpol. Even though he had only been seconded to the London bureau three months before, Cooper had quickly learned that Dakin was feared and respected in equal measures. He was also dogged in his investigations. However, one in particular had eluded him for the best part of a decade: Philippe Le Grande had been one of the most notorious drug dealers of the early 1960s. Operating mostly from Paris, Le Grande had commanded a network of drug trafficking that stretched across Europe. Never quite able to get enough evidence that would stick, Dakin had been slowly infiltrating Le Grande's inner circle. By 1966, a crook close to Le Grande was almost ready to squeal. Dakin had managed to guarantee the informer immunity and a new passport to South America. About a week before Le Grande was due to be arrested, he had died in a fire in a grotty flat above one of the many bars he ran as a centre to launder his drug money. Any number of rivals could have taken Le Grande out, Dakin knew, but to lose the opportunity to put him on trial so close to the day when he was going to snare him had haunted Dakin. Cooper knew that Dakin needed some closure on the whole Le Grande affair. Finding out who had killed him would not make the world a safer place – if anything, whoever had killed Le Grande had done the world a massive favour. But Dakin needed answers. He was due to retire later that year, and Cooper knew that he needed to draw a line under the whole matter. It went beyond the job, for Dakin. Cooper also knew that, if he gave Dakin what he needed, it would do his own career no harm at all. Dakin was not liked generally, but he was respected greatly – that counted for everything.

'What now?'

'We have a date – tonight.' Cooper waited for Dakin to shout at him for going too fast. However, to his surprise, Dakin almost allowed a note of pleasure to filter into his reply:

'Well, at least you're not letting the grass grow under your feet. Keep it cool. I will need to names of your contact and her friend to check them out this end.'

'I will have all that for you after tonight. But you won't find anything on my contact. A privately educated girl having fun before she has to grow up and get a proper life, I think. Doesn't know how easy she's had it. I imagine the friend is similar. I will speak to you again tomorrow. Same time?'

'Of course you bloody will!'

And with that, Dakin hung up again. Cooper allowed himself another wink at his own reflection before he left the phone booth. He had spotted a barber's shop across the street. A trim and a shave would start the day nicely, he thought. After all, he had to look his best for his date with Ava.

As Cooper was shaved and spruced into an even more handsome variant of himself, Ava was busily scooting between one boutique and another in the centre of Hanover. Normally a late sleeper, Satine had laughed as her friend had been up and out in time for the opening of the shops. Left alone, Satine had enjoyed a quiet morning. The call home this week had at least been full of genuine news about the photo shoot and the burgeoning creation of Mixed Emotions as a reality. Her mother had not sounded so convinced owing to the passing of yet another week, but Satine had become adept at putting on a positive spin after her initial wobble. She did feel genuinely optimistic and it was with delight that she found herself welcoming Claude into the apartment a few minutes after she had ended her call home.

'You don't mind me dropping by? Rosie said it would be okay.' Claude's soft French accent was as beautiful as his face, Satine decided. His command of English was as perfect as she had come to expect since she had been in Hanover. Keen to improve her own German, Satine found herself thwarted by the fact that everyone she encountered would speak perfect English the moment they knew where she was from – with the exception of some hostile shop proprietors, naturally. Satine knew that the UK was lagging behind in terms of the tuition of other languages, but being in Hanover really brought it home. She knew that there was a mentality where the British expected other nations would speak English and it made them lazy.

'I think it is nice to be dressed properly,' Claude said as they sat and shared a pot of coffee. He wore a simple T-shirt and jeans but they served to accentuate the beauty of his physique. He had slicked his curls back that morning, and his face had a youthful glow that lit up the room. He was at the stage in his life where he was the most beautiful mixture of handsome adulthood but with the freshness of youth.

'I think you came off worse! Were you cold?'

'I grew up on a farm – I am more tough than I look, I think.' Claude shared readily the story of his life with Satine, and the two found a very easy rapport. He was born into a farming family in Toulouse, the youngest of three boys. The older two now ran the farm, their parents having stepped back. Claude had felt alienated from that life from an early age, the macho and gruff nature of the farming community at odds with him. Escape to Paris. Then Amsterdam. Now Hanover. Like Ava and Satine, he had been acting and singing in various shows but the big break had yet to come.

'Do you keep in touch with your family?' Satine knew that this was a delicate question. Claude did not need to announce his sexuality, and Satine was prepared for a story that she had heard many times before. She was pleasantly surprised when Claude said:

'Oh yes, every week! They would have liked me to be on the farm, for sure, but they love me. They knew that life was not for me. I think that they think I will get this...stuff out of my system and become a farmer one day.' By 'stuff', Satine was not sure if he meant show business or homosexuality, or both. Reading her thoughts, Claude laughed:

'They know I am gay! It's okay. You are surprised?'

'Well,' Satine desperately didn't want to sound like she was making assumptions. 'It's just, you know, rural communities can be old-fashioned. There is a lot of prejudice back home.'

'Oh, prejudice is everywhere. Against people like me. Against you, no? Sometimes.'

'That's true enough.'

'But family is family. They don't ask too much, but when I need to go home, they are there!' Claude made it all sound so simple, Satine thought. Maybe he was lucky or had learned to view life in the simple way that he did. His positivity was refreshing, and she found herself liking Claude more and more. Yes, things were looking up, Satine thought.

Ava returned with a completely new outfit and spent the rest of the afternoon prepping herself for the date with Glen Cooper. Claude had excused himself shortly after she had returned, sensing that Satine would be called upon to give Ava her undivided attention. It had proved to be the case, as Ava changed into her new clothes and back into older, more trusted outfits with increasing panic. Eventually, she decided to take everything back to the shops and start again. Exhausted by the process, Satine dozed on the sofa and was only roused when Ava returned with a completely new set of clothes. Satine stirred groggily and noticed that her throat was sore, but she rallied herself enough to announce round two of the new outfit a great improvement on the first purchases. Mollified, Ava took to the bathroom and Satine found that she was crushed with fatigue. She dragged herself to her bed and pulled the covers around her without undressing.

When she awoke, the flat was in darkness and she was alone. Her throat was now raw with pain and her head felt like it had been crushed in a vice. She blundered into the lounge area, squinting at the note Ava had left her that said 'Couldn't wake you! See you later xx and then began searching for some paracetamol. Finding a full packet, she quickly downed two and staggered back to her bed. Managing (just) to undress this time, Satine slid under the covers and back into a deep sleep – a sleep that was populated with the strangest dreams that only an incipient fever could produce.

The restaurant that Cooper had booked for himself and Ava was one of the most expensive in the city. However, the credit card would be cleared via the office and he had to support the story he had used about his lucrative work in Australia. The credit card had also found its way into the hands of a very obsequious gentleman's outfitter assistant who had helped Cooper select the new suit he was wearing. This purchase might raise a few eyebrows in the accounts department, he knew, but he was more than capable of justifying the expenses with the charm he knew worked very well on the two ladies who signed off the expense claims each month. Besides, he felt that a suit worthy of James Bond was more than appropriate considering the work he was doing. He checked his watch (not a new one, but claimed on a previous assignment) and noticed that Ava was ten minutes late. A flash of concern brought the image of Dakin's angry face into his mind's eye, but he quickly chased the spectre away when he recalled how perfectly he had played things with Ava the night before.

Ava was not actually late to the restaurant. In fact, she had arrived half an hour early as she was still unsure of how long to allow to travel into the city centre in the evenings. Nights off up until now had usually been spent in the flat. Ava had walked past the restaurant three times until she noticed her date arriving and taking a seat at a table near the front of the glass-fronted and very elegant restaurant. She forced herself to circle the block one more time to ensure that she was just a little late, but could not help but giggle as she observed Cooper had been to the barbers and was wearing what looked like a new and stylish suit of grey flannel. She took a quick detour into the bathroom and added just a little more lipstick before announcing herself to the maître'd who showed her to the correct table. The handsome Australian grinned, flashing the perfect teeth that seemed to be even whiter against his tanned complexion, and jumped to his feet as she walked towards him. He kissed her gently on the cheek, wasting no time in telling her how gorgeous she looked.

'This place looks wonderful' Ava cast her eyes around the opulent room which was full of very rich-looking diners and allowed herself a moment to drink in the surroundings. A string quartet played in a corner of the room. One wall was almost entirely occupied by a huge fish tank, with an array of exquisitely hued creatures floating back and forth.

'Only the best for a beautiful woman.' Cooper peered into Ava's eyes and smiled. 'I took the liberty of ordering some wine. Is red okay for you?'

'Yes, my favourite!' Ava lied. Ava was really only a white wine drinker, but whatever this handsome man had selected would be more than fine. The wine came almost immediately, and Cooper declared his offered tasting sample to be 'wonderful.' To her delight, the wine was indeed delicious. Ava had been put off red wine in England because it was usually vile, but this tasted completely unlike anything she had tasted back home. It was even nicer than anything she had sampled on holiday in France, but he knew that the company was playing its part in making everything seem just that bit more special.

'So, I think I bored you with my work story last time. Tonight I want to hear all about Mixed….Feelings?'

'Emotions. Mixed Emotions.' Ava corrected him.

'Sorry. Mixed Emotions. My mistake.' Cooper smiled away his error. It was, of course, no error at all but he did not want Ava to think that his interest in her silly little pop group was anything but part of his genuine desire to find out everything about the beautiful woman before him. The fact that it was the only thing he was really interested in at all called for some careful handling. But he was definitely the man for the job. As he saw Ava's eyes light up at what she took to be his genuine interest, he knew that he was playing things beautifully.

As the night went on, Ava would share all the information she had on Mixed Emotions and its members. It was not nearly enough at this stage, but Cooper would report back to Dakin the following morning that all was going well. He would not even allow himself to be anything but the perfect gentleman and refuse the offer of coming up to her flat for a coffee when their shared taxi reached her place. He couldn't help but chuckle as he thought about the disappointed look that had flashed in her eyes, only to be replaced by dewy contentment that she had clearly met a man who was out for more than sex.

Sex was very much on Cooper's mind as the taxi drove away from Ava's apartment and he instructed the driver to take him to a lively part of town. He also found himself chuckling when he realised that the woman he did take back to his dingy hotel that evening was not at all, unlike Ava in appearance. Sex with the real Ava would have to wait until he got the goods on Cicely. Ava was in a great place to give him everything Dakin would need Cooper to provide, but she was nowhere near as useful as she would need to be yet. But he could wait.

It was morning when Satine next became aware of anything. Ava had left her a cup of coffee next to her bed at some point, but it was now stone cold. Satine could not have even sipped it anyway as her throat felt like it had broken glass in it and the headache was unspeakably painful. She tried to swing her legs to the floor and rise, but the effort was too much and she fell back with a loud groan. This alerted Ava who was in the lounge.

'Are you okay, honey?' Ava sat on the bed next to Satine and instinctively placed her palm on her friend's brow. 'My God! You are burning up!'

'I feel like death!' Satine's voice came out as a low growl and she winced with the effort.

'Shall I get someone? Weiler? A doctor?'

'No,' Satine grumbled, 'no fuss. Just let me sleep. Maybe some more pills.'

Frowning, Ava fetched Satine some more paracetamol and a large glass of water. Satine downed the tablets with a gulp of the water and almost immediately fell back into a doze. Worry compelled Ava to head for the door of the flat to rouse Weiler, despite what Satine had said. However, she was just about to open the door when it flew open itself, nearly hitting her in the face. Bemused, she staggered back as Rosie burst into the flat, Weiler behind her.

'You're here! Thank God!' Rosie swept past her and came to a halt in the centre of the lounge area. Her eyes darted around the room. 'Where's Satine?' She barked this angrily.

'She's in bed….she's sick..' Ava tried to regain her composure, but Rosie was on the move again – this time actually pushing Ava aside as she stalked towards Satine's bedroom.

'Sick? Sick! She can't be sick!' Rosie thundered as she wrenched open the door to Satine's bedroom. She disappeared into the room, slamming the door behind her in anger. Dumbfounded and now angry, Ava spun round to Weiler and demanded:

'What the Hell is going on? Satine is sick! I was just about to get you to call a doctor.'

Weiler looked awkward and there was obvious concern in his voice when he replied.

'Sick? My God, yes, of course – I will get her a doctor. But, I think this is very bad timing for Rosie as –' Weiler's words were cut off as Rosie sprang from Satine's bedroom and began circling the lounge carpet in obvious panic.

'She is sick!' She said this to nobody in particular. 'Damn it! Shiesse!' She continued a tirade in German, using words that Ava had not heard before but were obviously enough to clear a dockside bar. After a few moments where Rosie stood stock still, only her eyes darting furiously back and forth. Suddenly, she seemed to orientate back into action. She barked:

'Weiler! Get her a doctor!'

Without a further word, Weiler spun on his heels and headed for his own flat.

'This is terrible!' Rosie spat. For a second, Ava thought that she was seeing genuine concern for her friend's health and wondered if Satine had become suddenly even worse in the moments it had taken for Rosie to enter and exit the bedroom. Then, seeing the hard look in Rosie's eyes, she knew that the primary concern was not Satine. Unprompted, Rosie looked Ava squarely in the face and spoke with breakneck rapidity, clearly deciding her actions as she went along:

'Right. Weiler will get her a doctor and stay here with Satine. You! Get in the car. Cicely is at the club already with Claude but we need you now! Go! Schnell!'

'What?!' Ava found her voice and her anger at the same time. 'I'm not going to leave Satine until the doctor gets here! Why do you want me to go anyway?' Rosie glared at Ava, but the determination in Ava's voice was clear.

Forcing herself to soften slightly, Rosie held up her hand and waved it in a placatory manner.

'Weiler will look after Satine. It's okay.'

'It is not okay!' Ava almost screamed, pushing past Rosie and opening the door to Satine's bedroom. Satine was motionless and seemed to be asleep, despite the histrionics unfolding all around her which only made Ava more worried. However, just as she was about to try and rouse Satine, Weiler returned to the flat with news that the doctor had been called and would be with them immediately.

'I am not going anywhere until I know what the doctor says.' Ava said slowly and fixed Rosie with an unflinching stare as she spoke each word. The corners of Rosie's mouth twitched as if she was about the explode again, but seemed to decide against it. She held up her hand again and nodded sharply.

'What is all this about anyway?' Ava said after a seemingly endless silence.

'We have to go to the club. There is a photoshoot this afternoon.' Weiler answered for Rosie.

'First, we've heard about it! We already did one, remember – weeks ago. Not that anything has come of it yet!' Rosie seemed to be poised to react to this last statement but decided against it. When she answered Ava, she had managed to switch back into her usual cloying and slightly robotic demeanour:

'S.K. got a call late last night. *Sounds Now* offered him three pages and a shoot with one of their best photographers – Gunter Brine.' Rosie clearly expected the name of the photographer to mean something to Ava, but she just shrugged. However, the title of the magazine was familiar to Ava. *Sounds Now* was a music bible, published across Europe. Some of Rosie's excitement and panic was justified. Weiler interjected again, and Ava was aware that he was genuinely trying to keep Rosie at bay for the sake of both herself and Satine.

'S.K. called in some favours with the editor, but the deal is that the shoot gets done today. No second chances.'

'Well…. all well and good,' Ava looked challengingly at Rosie, 'but Satine is not going anywhere – regardless of what the doctor says.'

Rosie made no comment but rather took to one of the stools at the breakfast bar and seemed to go into another reverie. She was clearly thinking her way around this problem, but it seemed insurmountable to Ava.

With typical German efficiency, the doctor arrived within fifteen minutes. Satine was diagnosed as having a mild bug that bed rest and fluids would sort out in about twenty- four hours. As Weiler showed the doctor out, Ava expected another Vesuvius-style eruption from Rosie at the prospect of losing the *Sounds Now* opportunity. To her surprise, Rosie merely said:

'Okay, so now we know. Weiler will take us to the club and then return here to look after Satine. She will be fine.'

'But how can we –'

'Please! No more questions!' Rosie glanced at her watch. ' We will be okay as long as we go now. Yes?' She looked imploringly at Ava, clearly terrified that she was going to refuse.

'I will come straight back here – half an hour at the most until I am back. Yes?' Weiler actually took Ava by the hand as he said this and nodded reassuringly. 'Yes?'

'Yes.' Ava replied at length.

Ten minutes later, Weiler had got them within a few blocks of the club. The route had become very familiar to Ava over the last few weeks, so she was very surprised when Rosie suddenly barked an order for Weiler to take a turn away from the direction of the club. Weiler quizzed Rosie in German and was given a hasty answer, after which he complied with the instruction.

Ava watched as the car moved along increasingly grimy streets as they headed across the town. Her geography of Hanover had started to piece together and she knew that the club was about a mile away from the main shopping areas. Between the club and the more wholesome city attractions like the museums, restaurants, and shopping arcades was the red light district. Quiet in the daytime, the streets still ticked over with the steady trickle of cars crawling towards the obvious sex workers that loitered on litter-strewn street corners. The screamingly obvious cars belonging to the pimps were always nearby, their windows shaded but ever watchful.

Bemused, Ava could only watch in awed silence as Rosie instructed Weiler to park the Mercedes behind one of the most obvious of the shaded cars. Wordlessly, Weiler complied and Rosie promptly got out of the car and marched to the driver's window of the pimp mobile as confidently as if she had been going into a general store for a carton of orange juice. The window lowered but Ava could not see the inhabitant from where she was sitting.

She could see Rosie remonstrating with someone, and after a few minutes, she saw Rosie reach into her pocket and take out a large wad of cash. A hairy hand decorated with thick gold rings plucked the money from her and the window was closed again. Rosie straightened up, turning from the car to look over to the opposite side of the street. Following her gaze, Ava saw that there were three women clustered near a telephone box. Clearly working girls, they were dressed in short skirts and tight tops, with fishnet stockings and ridiculously high-heeled shoes. As with their attitude to pornography, Ava could only smile at the frankness of the German approach to prostitution in comparison to the British. Two of the women were white, the local blonde colouring accentuated with brash peroxide dye to their bouffant manes. The third was a black, taller, and willowy figure. Her hair (a rather ratty wig) was long and straight. Like her fellows, the woman was striking but with an unmistakable harshness about her face. Ava could only wonder what her life experiences had been. Rosie pointed at the black woman, inclining her head towards the pimp's car. Immediately, the woman strutted across the road and stood at the driver's window, just as Rosie had done minutes before. The window lowered again and the woman nodded as she was given her instructions.

Ava was convinced she must have been in a state of hallucination as Rosie climbed back into the car and the prostitute slid onto the passenger seat next to Ava. The woman smelled of cigarettes and a cloyingly sweet perfume. Close up, Ava could see that the wig had slipped back to reveal a fuzzy hairline and that there were dark rings under the heavily made-up eyes. The woman looked mildly at the bemused Ava and said:

'Candy.'

Ava had no idea what to say in reply to Candy's introduction, but fortunately, the air was immediately filled by Rosie who barked:

'For the next two hours, you answer to the name of Satine if you are spoken to at all. And you don't start a conversation with anyone.'

Candy grunted, clearly unphased by either Rosie's orders or the tone with which they were delivered. She had clearly heard a lot worse.

Ava contemplated several things that she might have said as Weiler drove them to the club, but each time the words died in her throat as she realised that there were some situations for which there were no words.

The rest of the afternoon was a haze for Ava. Claude and Cicely were already kitted out in the awful clothes from the previous shoot when Ava arrived at the club. She dressed hastily into her own ensemble in the ladies' room, Candy by her side as she donned Satine's clothes. Rosie had judged Candy's size well, but an additional feather boa was needed to hide the way the outfit gaped in some places and was a little too snug in others. Claude was as flabbergasted as Ava, but Cicely seemed to take everything in her stride and behaved like an actor in a soap opera whose co-star had just been swapped for another player but carried on as if nothing had happened. Mercifully, Candy was provided with a new and much better wig by Rosie within about an hour. Once she had confirmed with Rosie that she did not have to give the new wig back afterward, Candy pulled the threadbare piece from her head and dumped it straight in the nearest bin. Ava hoped that the wig would not try to bite any of the cleaners that night.

The celebrated Gunter Brine was as taciturn and aloof as S.K. A slight wisp of a man with a shaved head and a huge moustache, he had an entourage of gophers to whom he whispered instructions and it was they who actually spoke to the four as they arranged them in various poses. Perversely, next to Cicely, it was Candy/Satine who seemed the most relaxed and it became clear that an afternoon in a warm club posing for photos was a pleasant change to how she would usually spend the time. The make-up artist was noticeably better than Rumpelstiltskin had been and Ava actually felt like this shoot was more what she had imagined – once she shut out the obvious fact that her best friend had been replaced with a hooker!

The shoot ended within two hours, S.K. and Rosie swanning off with the 'wonderful' Gunter Brine to do the *Sounds Now* interview at the recording studio. Cicely had been chosen by Rosie to accompany them to give a few soundbites on behalf of the group. This surprised neither Ava nor Claude, as once again, it was clear that Cicely was being arranged in the photographs as the main focus.

When her taxi dropped her off, Ava was relieved to see that Weiler had stayed the whole time with Satine. The invalid had slept throughout the afternoon, Weiler informed Ava, but by the evening she was delighted when Satine migrated to the sofa. She looked drawn, but the worst had obviously passed.

'I was so out of it earlier,' Satine said, 'and I didn't ask you about your date.'

'Oh, it was great.' Ava paused. 'Yeah, really great.'

'You don't sound so sure.'

'Oh, no! Glen was lovely. Really. It's just that what happened today kind of knocked last night off the map a bit.' Ava knew the big explanation of the events that Satine had slept through was needed, but even now she felt like she had been subject to a dream of her own.

'So…what did happen today?' Satine pulled her robe around her and leaned forward, intrigue chasing away the tiredness that she still felt.

Ava took a large gulp of the white wine she had poured. Where to begin?

Chapter Six – 'Mr Dead.'

Rosie clucked and clapped her hands delightedly as she laid the photograph proofs out on the large conference table in the downstairs room of the recording studio. Satine, Ava, Cicely, and Claude stood around the table as each image was placed to Rosie's growing glee.

'He is a genius! This is gold! Pure gold!' she cooed. And it had to be said that Gunter Brine certainly deserved his reputation and the huge salary that *Sounds Now* no doubt paid him for his work. Even the costumes looked better and the post-production had rendered the club into a sea of light and mist.

'Fantastic.'

Satine did nothing to disguise her contempt as she glowered at the images of Candy.

'Now, now, now!' Rosie's mood was not going to be lowered by anyone and she breezily patted Satine on the hand in the patronising manner that had become her hallmark. 'We did what we could in the time we had! The shots we have already will go on the record sleeve, so relax.'

'And when will that be?' This was from Claude. The quietest of them all in the rare group gatherings, even Claude was reaching the end of his patience. The impromptu photoshoot notwithstanding, there had still been nothing to indicate that Mixed Emotions would actually have a product to slip into a record sleeve.

'Aha!' Rosie was like a satanic Mary Poppins and Satine wondered if she had taken barbiturates with her scrambled eggs that morning. 'The wait is almost over! That, aside from unveiling these fabulous pictures, is what we are here for today! S.K. is on his way over with our first song! We start recording this very afternoon!'

Both Satine and Ava let out a little gasp of excitement when Rosie said this and Claude whooped. Only Cicely kept her composure, managing a soft but genuine grin at the news.

'Details?' Ava asked.

'Mixed Emotions! Written by S.K. himself!'

'But that's our name – Mixed Emotions. What's the song called?' This time it was Satine who spoke. Rosie looked at her with supremely patronising patience.

'Yes – you are. So is the song! Mixed Emotions by Mixed Emotions.'

'That sounds a bit….obvious.' Cicely covered the sedition in her words with another grin. Rosie seemed on the brink of unleashing the beast that they all knew lurked close to the surface, but she paused and the rage stopped at the tightened corners of the mouth in the manner they had all become quite accustomed to recognising. Claude, Satine and Ava all knew that Rosie would only dial back her instinctive nastiness owing to the fact that it had been Cicely who denounced the idea as 'obvious.'

'Not 'obvious' Cicely…dear.' The last word was rendered as an expletive by the tone Rosie struck when she intoned it. 'Mixed Emotions by Mixed Emotions is a stroke of marketing genius. Everyone will know the song and never forget the name of the band! Genius!'

With that, Rosie swept out of the room and headed up the stairs to the recording studio. When they were sure she was out of earshot, Mixed Emotions mulled the true 'genius' of this decision.

'Doesn't that idea have 'one hit wonder' written all over it?' Satine asked. 'If we are so firmly identified with the first song, how do we move on to anything else?'

'I agree with you,' Claude frowned. 'It seems like a mistake.'

'Mistake or not,' Cicely replied, 'they have made their minds up. This will be S.K.'s idea and his alone. Rosie couldn't wipe her own arse without his instructions on how to do it. Even then, he will insist on seeing the evidence before he lets her do it a second time.'

Delivered in such a matter- of- fact tone, Satine and the others found themselves still laughing half an hour later when a bemused Rosie returned to the room to tell them that it was time to go up to the recording studio.

S.K. did not communicate with any of them directly or speak anything other than German throughout the recording session, but none of the Mixed Emotions could fail but be impressed by the sheer technical genius by which he worked the massive mixing desks. He played the desks like they were finely tuned musical instruments in themselves, which they began to realise was actually very much the case. Every piece of instrumentation had been pre-recorded or created from scratch by the machinery. A turned dial here, a flicked switch there and a whole orchestra of sound could be issued, changed and issued again. Rosie relayed S.K.'s orders in her usual frenetic manner, clapping her hands as she chased the members to the booth when it was their turn like she was rounding up wayward chickens in a farmer's yard.

It surprised neither Ava, Satine or Claude that Cicely was given the first spot in the recording booth. They had all been given the lyrics of the song 'Mixed Emotions', which all four had privately concluded were trite and unimpressive. Knowing that their opinion was not going to be sought, they communicated with the odd eye roll whenever S.K. or Rosie were not looking. Reassuringly for Ava and Satine, Cicely rolled her eyes as much as anyone else. There seemed to be a sense of the four bonding through a shared appraisal of the material as being 'merde' (as Claude bravely whispered at one point whilst S.K. and Rosie were in close discussion at the other end of the room.

Cicely was required to sing an opening refrain, which Rosie said S.K. wanted to be acapella before the disco beat kicked in and the whole group would add their vocals. In the booth, Cicely was instructed to sing over and over the lyrics that sounded even more unimpressive as they became familiar:

'These mixed emotions are killing me.

Trapped so deep now I just can't see.

Love me or leave me baby

But show me you heart or a way back to me.'

This last line seemed to Ava and Satine to be the most clumsy, but Cicely actually managed to put the line across so that it rendered a sense of pain. Equally, there was no doubting that her voice was both clear and powerful. Her breath control spoke of someone who had honed their craft and the style of her singing was extremely accomplished. When Ava and then Satine were tasked with singing their own sections, they were first instructed to sing the lines 'killing me' and 'set me free' over and over which were to be placed underneath Cicely's main vocal. Relieved to actually start singing, both women made the best of it and were actually pleased when Rosie passed on the message from S.K .that they were 'lovely singers.' This pleased Ava the most as it was the first time anyone had asked her to sing a note. Claude was given the least to do, but eventually all four had sung their way through the entire song. Claude's voice was reedy but sweet. After about four hours, Rosie announced that their work was done and it was time for S.K. to 'make magic and alchemy.' The great man himself managed to grunt his approval as they filed out of the upstairs room, waving a thumbs up at them all and even blowing Cicely a kiss.

'He's not dying, is he?' Satine whispered to Ava as they descended the stairs. 'That was almost an acknowledgment that we are human beings!'

Claude and Cicely were sent off in taxis, leaving Ava and Satine to wait for Weiler to collect them. Rosie had informed them all that there would be no club work that evening and both women were surprised how exhausting the day had been and looked forward to the prospect of long baths and an early night. When Weiler sounded the car horn to announce his arrival, Ava went directly out to the waiting vehicle. Satine took a few minutes to use the bathroom and, as she exited the building towards Weiler's waiting car, she was more than a little delighted to see Lukas trotting along the pavement towards the studio. Waving enthusiastically, Lukas flashed the dimpled grin that always lifted her spirits.

'Hey you!' Lukas beamed, kissing her cheek and then looking immediately very bashful which delighted Satine. Could he get any cuter?

'I'm just going. This is bad timing!'

'I know, what a pain!' Lukas shrugged.' S.K. wants me here now to mix the song. It will probably take all night, knowing him.'

'Well,' Satine leaned towards him and whispered, 'best of luck with that! The song is crap!'

Lukas giggled shyly, his eyes darting back and forth to check that neither S.K. or Rosie were around before he replied:

'Between you and me, they usually are at this stage. But the guy is actually a genius despite the hype that Rosie puts around. It will be great when we're finished. I promise.'

Before Satine could reply, Weiler blasted his car horn impatiently and she excused herself, trotting towards the waiting Mercedes. Nevertheless, she noticed that Lukas paused in the doorway of the studio and watched as they were driven away. The dimpled grin lit up the doorway.

Buzzing, Ava and Satine sat up late into the night, drinking wine and daring to believe that this was the true start of what they had come to Hanover for in the first place. Before they had settled into their cups, Satine had made her weekly call to her mother, delighted that she was able to say that she had recorded a pop song. Naturally, she left out the part about a prostitute taking her place at a photoshoot and glossed over her sudden illness as 'something she ate' that took her out of action for a day. Iodine seemed mollified that a doctor had been summoned very promptly and that her baby girl was clearly 'treasured as she should be and looked after well.' Thinking back to the way that Weiler had attended to her throughout the day until Ava returned, she did not find it was at all difficult to agree. Although, had it not been for Ava, Satine was pretty sure that Rosie would have tried to force her to the photoshoot.

They awoke slightly hungover but with the warm buzz of expectation that the day would bring news of the single being mixed and ready to press. Performances would surely follow in places outside of the wretched Kasbah and then the press junkets would begin in earnest. However, that day passed without any news. Then the next. And the next. The days became a week, and each time one or the other of them tried to bring the topic up with Rosie, she smiled it away and said that S.K. was 'immersed in the process.' Lukas confirmed that S.K. had worked him solidly through the entire night and most of the next day and finally announced that he was satisfied. But even Lukas had not been able to hear the complete mix, having been eventually dismissed bleary-eyed from the studio as S.K. announced that the last stages would be completed by himself alone. Apparently, this was not unusual as S.K. guarded his product very jealously. He had (according to Rosie) fallen foul of copycats in the past who had taken his ideas and scored hits before S.K. stop them. Both Ava and Satine were sceptical when Rosie demurred at the request to elaborate.

The now typical routine lumbered on for the next few weeks, Satine and Ava working their usual shifts at the club, occasionally coinciding with Cicely. If she was growing as impatient as they were, Cicely kept a very tight lid on things. She had grown a little more communicative based on the fact that they at least had some shared experiences as Mixed Emotions now, but both Ava and Satine were always aware of a cut-off point in conversation; Cicely listened patiently and with apparent interest as they unfolded anecdotes about their lives and experiences but never volunteered anything about herself that they did not already know.

The club itself had become much busier since Ava and Satine had started working there. Several new dancers had started performing, although Lotte and Tamara still got the prime slots when the club was at its most packed and they were by far the most popular. They were performing twice as often on the busiest evenings and their podiums were practically hidden under drifts of bank notes – all of which were expertly rounded up by Rosie. Nevertheless, their cut was clearly more substantial as Tamara began to wax lyrical about how much she was starting to build up 'a nice little bundle for my babies.' Satine had been surprised by Lotte in the manner with which she spoke about Rosie as they sat after hours waiting for their taxis one Friday night:

'She seems to have found her reasonable side. We are getting about a third more each night than before. If this keeps up, I might even stick around until the Spring.'

'Were you planning on going sooner? We'd miss you!' Satine had come to look forward to her late night chats with Lotte, especially when she got her perfectly straight, white teeth into Rosie.

'I am going home for a few days at Christmas. I toyed with the idea of making it permanent. Now,' Lotte shrugged, 'I think I might stay a bit longer. Tamara is desperate to get back home in time for her youngest's birthday in March.'

'She'd miss you if you went before her.'

'Oh, I know,' Lotte smiled. 'She says that she finds it so much easier if I am up there beside her – she can tune the rest out. Anyway,' her eyes scanned the room to locate Rosie; she nodded contentedly when she saw that Rosie was leaning at the bar and in conversation with some of the regulars and beyond earshot. 'I am curious about her sudden generosity. She's happy about something.'

'I hope it's Mixed Emotions,' Satine frowned, 'although the longer this drags on, the more I doubt it is ever going to get going.'

'Hold your nerve there,' Lotte advised. 'S.K. is a bastard, but he's a clever one. If he went to the effort to get you all together in the first place, then he won't let it come to nothing. Madame Rosie acts like she knows what S.K. is up to but she knows shit when it comes down to it – he just drip feeds her what he wants her to know when she can be of use.'

Hoping she was right, Satine tried to keep Lotte's words in her mind as the nights at the club merged into each other. As the routine of spilling their way into profit for the club became second-nature, Ava and Satine began to operate alone at times as they no longer felt the need for joint effort in fleecing the unsuspecting drunks that Rosie placed in their paths. This, inevitably, lead to periods where one or the other of them were free to drift around the club. Conversation with Rosie soon grew tiresome as she would never be drawn on what Ava and Satine really wanted to discuss – Mixed Emotions. Satine was convinced that, as usual, Lotte had been completely correct in her appraisal of Rosie in that she was only privy to whatever S.K. decided she needed to know at any one time. Lukas was not at the club often for evening shifts, so Satine found that she began talking more to some of the regular patrons that frequented the Kasbah. Although men on business trips accounted for the majority of footfall, there were a small but strong number of locals who appeared one or twice a week. In particular, Satine found it an ideal opportunity to try an acquire more conversational German. This proved to be as frustrating as ever, as nearly every German she encountered in the club detected that she was English within seconds and conversed in (typically) clear English. However, there was one key exception to this rule and Satine found herself increasingly drawn to the company of a man that she had, initially, avoided like the plague…

Hans Heinrich Stiefel was a ghoulish animated cadaver of a man who stood over six feet tall with thick grey hair and a complexion to match. Immaculately dressed in beautifully tailored suits, always complete with a waistcoat and gold fob watch, Stiefel had acquired the title 'Mr Dead' by Lotte and it fitted the figure perfectly. His long, slender fingers were constantly entwined around an ivory cigarette holder and the hallow of smoke around him added to the sense that he had just been conjured up on the altar of a necromancer. His eyes were hooded and so dark as to repel light and enhance the impression in the deliberate gloom of the club that a skull as opposed to a face rested on his shoulders. The name 'Mr Dead' worked on two levels as, fittingly enough, Hans Heinrich Stiefel was an undertaker. Rosie fawned over Stiefel as he was fantastically rich. The Stiefel family had been burying the dead of Hanover for centuries and their business operated from the East wing of one of the biggest mansion houses in the city. It had survived the wartime bombing without so much as a tile being displaced when all around it had been decimated. This added to the local myth that the Stiefel's had ancestral links to Transylvania and Vlad the Impaler who had sold his soul to a vampire. Looking at Stiefel, Satine could see how such stories had flourished. If Hans carried a family resemblance, his entire family must have been terrifying small children, dogs, cats and the more nervous horses that passed the mansion gates for generations.

However, for all the undead aura, Satine had found herself pleasantly surprised by Stiefel after he had approached her one evening. Her companion for the night (a shoe manufacturer from Manchester on a buying trip) had been poured penniless into a taxi by Rosie's bouncers after he had managed to sink enough of the champagne that Satine had not 'accidentally' thrown on the floor down his fat neck and slide unconscious under the booth table. Deciding that she would finish the half bottle of champagne as a deserved treat for the seemingly endless hour she had spent being told about the 'fascinating' methods by which German shoe production was superior to the rest of Europe, Satine had not noticed Stiefel approach her until he stood by her side like a sentinel from Hades.

'May I join you for a time, madame? My name is Hans Heinrich Stiefel and I would very much enjoy the chance to converse with you. Rosie informs me that you are English. I would enjoy to converse as my spoken English is not yet perfected.'

Satine glanced sharply towards the bar, where Rosie stood and raised her glass to her as a sign that this was a task she expected Satine to perform. Forcing a smile as she strained her neck to look him in the eye, Satine replied:

'Herr Stiefel, please…' she nodded to the space opposite where she sat that had recently been occupied by the cobbling Manchunian. Stiefel nodded sharply and sat down.

'Rosie tells me you are Miss Satine. You are from London in England, yes?' He had a voice that was gentler and warm, belying the Hammer horror movie exterior. Satine noticed that, face to face, she could now actually see his eyes. They were brown and seemed kind, almost a little sad.

'Not originally, no, but Ava and I worked in the West End before coming here. If you are in the entertainment world, you really have to be in London if you want work.' Satine offered Stiefel some champagne, but he demurred.

'I will have some of my favourite wine sent over instead. I have Rosie keep a case of it chilled at all times. I think you will find it very acceptable.' He offered Satine a cigarette. When she refused, he suggested that he would refrain too. Satine assured him that she didn't mind him smoking (the club reeked of it at all times anyway) but she could not help but be touched by the considerate way in which he had sought her permission. Perhaps it was true that, with serious and old money came true class. When it arrived, the wine was the best that Satine could remember having tasted.

The rest of the evening flew by for Satine. Stiefel patiently translated words and phrases into German whenever Satine asked him to do so, rapidly learning to give bi-lingual commentaries on his anecdotes without being prompted. She often repeated phrases in German to check her understanding. If she erred even slightly, Stiefel corrected her without making any allowances. Although a little on edge with this approach at first, Satine soon realised that she rather liked his directness. After endless weeks contending with the mendacity of Rosie, Stiefel's demeanour was refreshing. And he was very interesting! At one point, Satine visited the bathroom and found that Ava had scurried after her to find out what was going on.

'You're drinking with Mr Dead!' Ava hissed amidst snorts of laughter. 'Rosie must have set that up!'

'Well, it was clearly her idea,' Satine found herself surprisingly defensive of Stiefel: 'But he's actually a really interesting guy. A gentleman, I think.'

'I'm going to put garlic around the windows tonight! Have we got a crucifix in the flat? Maybe Weiler might have one.' Ava roared with laughter.

'Don't! Seriously, he's okay.'

Seeing that Satine was not going to be drawn in, Ava shrugged and made her way back to the booth she had been spilling champagne over that evening. Her guest, an American toupee maker on a hair buying trip, was far from the point of collapse and was re-ordering bottles as fast as Ava could knock them sideways.

'So, have you always worked in the family business, Herr Stiefel?' Satine had found it sweet that, although she had invited him to call her just by her first name several times, it was clear that Stiefel was going to only refer to her as 'Miss Satine' and she was quite enjoying returning the respectful formality.

'Yes, Miss Satine. It is what I was born to do and my father taught me all from an early age. I went to university, of course, as one does but it was always inevitable that I would take the reins. It happened earlier than I imagined when father passed away before I graduated.'

'Sorry to hear that, Herr Stiefel. So is it just you….or..?'

'My mother has a partial interest in the day to day running of our service, but she is increasingly leaving it to me now. I have two apprentices. They are not without promise but….a little too interested in the living to be trusted to work with the dead without my supervision at all times.'

Satine wondered if she could label his delivery as 'deadpan' without it being too much of a cliché, but she couldn't help but find herself smiling at his reference to the poor apprentices who would rather be chatting up the mourners at a funeral than focusing on the star of the show. She toyed with her next question before asking it:

'Has the business left you time for….marriage?' This seemed a sensitive way of phrasing it. Stiefel clearly enjoyed women – why spent evenings in the Kasbah otherwise? It certainly wasn't for the wine (aside from the superior vintage he brought with him) and Rosie could hardly be a draw for anyone.

'No, Miss Simone. I think that, as you British say, the boat has sailed for me there.' He looked steadily at her as he said this, and Satine could see a brief flash of sadness that he quickly glossed over with his Germanic practicality. 'I enjoy my cars and my solitude. I think sharing good wine with a beautiful and talented lady is enough.'

Satine decided long before the end of the evening that she liked Stiefel. He was strange, but strange was rapidly becoming the norm. Satine had no idea how glad she would soon be to have made an acquaintance of Hans Heinrich Stiefel. Despite her amusement at the thought of it, Ava would be glad of it too.

Cooper had deliberately spaced out his dates with Ava as the first two were in such rapid succession that he was concerned he would lose control of the pace. He had elected for a couple of daytime meetings, taking in a 'romantic' river trip and a matinee of some old British Film that was showing at an art house cinema called 'Brief Encounter.' Ava had cried through it, announcing about twenty times that it was one of her favourites. Cooper had held Ava's tightly when the clipped pom had decided to do the 'right thing' and not leave her husband. He found the whole thing even duller and more pointless than he had expected, but it was all grist to the mill. The movie had given him some valuable thinking time as he tuned out the monochrome, over-coated angst that played out on grimy train station platforms. Dakin had been on blistering form that morning, nearly melting the receiver of the phone as he denounced Cooper as a 'lazy fucking Aussie' who was clearly only fit for 'shagging, drinking crap beer and losing at cricket.' The last insult was the only one that penetrated

Cooper's hide, and he was determined that he would get the goods for Dakin sooner rather than later. With this in mind, he turned the conversation to Cicely as they drank their coffee in a small café opposite the cinema as the day began to dip into night.

'So, have you heard the recording yet? When is it out?'

'Not a thing yet. Rosie keeps fobbing us off, saying S.K. has to line up as many radio stations and television spots as he can in advance or the single will just stay on the shelves.' Ava shrugged. 'Satine and I are fed up, but what can you do? We've come this far, we don't have much option but to wait. S.K. seems to know what he's doing.'

'And…are the others of the same mind? What about… Claude and…?' Cooper let his voice drop, deliberately leaving out Cicely's name.

'Cicely. Well, Claude, he's about the same as us about it all. Fed up, but Rosie has got him doing gopher work for S.K. and he has a decent apartment too. He's biding his time. Cicely…well, who knows?'

'What do you mean?' Cooper congratulated himself on the way he was steering Ava.

'Cicely keeps to herself. She's pleasant enough, but I don't think I know her any better now than I did when we first met.' Ava thought for a moment, then continued: 'Satine chats to her when they coincide at the club, which isn't that often. I think she feels pretty much the same about her really.'

'Don't you think that maybe you should try and get to know her a bit better?' Cooper bit his lip in frustration as he realised this had been blunt. He could almost hear Dakin hissing abuse in his ear along the lines of 'nice one, Hercule fucking Poirot' or something similar.

'Why?' He didn't care for the way that Ava was arching her eyebrow. Some of the dewy eyed look she usually gave him seemed to sharpen. He reminded himself that, smitten though she clearly was, Ava was no idiot.

'Well, I just think that maybe you should try and get under her skin a bit. She's part of Mixed Emotions and...' he floundered for a moment but then found his feet: 'you said yourself that S.K. had made her look like the star in the pictures. And she sang the lead vocals on the song. If she's planning on checking out, that could be a big deal for all of you – especially at this stage.'

Cooper could have leapt to the glass behind Ava and kissed his own handsome reflection.

'God…you're right.' Ava mulled this over for a moment, playing idly with the spoon on her saucer. 'I think we really need to find out what she is really thinking about everything. If she's thinking of walking-'

'I didn't say that!'

'Oh, I know you didn't. But, we have to make sure that Cicely wants the same things we do. Everything seems so up in the air as it is with S.K. and Rosie. We can at least work on strengthening us as a group.'

'My point exactly.' Cooper gave Ava his best, dazzling smile. He had it on good authority that the way his face creased up around his eyes accentuated his masculine charm when he smiled. He held it until it threatened to become a rictus. 'Hey! Here's a plan: why don't you and Satine invite Cicely for dinner. You know, just the girls hanging out together.'

'Claude might feel a bit excluded' Ava frowned, 'but if we invited them both to the apartment…'

'That sounds perfect!'

'Yes,' Ava smiled contentedly. 'I think it is a great idea. Thank you, Glen.'

Oh no, thought Cooper. Thank you.

Ava had to work at the club that evening, as Cooper had already been very careful to ascertain before suggesting the date. Her beauty made it very easy to whisper that he wished he could spend the rest of the day with her as they kissed their farewells outside her apartment. The sexual chemistry between them was definitely fizzing. It continued to fizz as he trotted off to his now familiar collection of bars where he knew the night could be rounded off in a way that was suitably rewarding for the sterling work he had done that afternoon.

Chapter Seven – Be Careful What You Wish For….

The next week dragged by for Satine and Ava with nothing from Rosie but her usual evasion. Ava had been particularly down in the dumps because Glen Cooper had told her that he would be travelling out of the city for most of the week to inspect signal systems in the countryside as part of his training. Satine knew that her friend was completely smitten with the handsome Australian and expected that Ava would mope around until the weekend when he said he would have more time. However, Ava rallied herself with elaborate plans for the dinner party that they had invited Claude and Cicely to attend that Wednesday. Claude had accepted like a flash, which did not surprise either Ava or Satine. Cicely's warm and immediate acceptance surprised them a little, but it certainly seemed to confirm that it was the right thing to do. Ava did not share with Satine that the idea had initially been suggested by Cooper, not wanting her friend to think that she was being told what to think by this new man in her life. Ava had always worn her heart on her sleeve, she knew, but even she worried about the extent to which she was falling for Cooper. For her part, Satine was not unduly concerned for Ava but was still reserving judgement on

Cooper until she got to know him better. Ava was like the sister that she had never had and Satine knew that she would always be very protective of her, whoever the man and however gorgeous he was or seemed. In terms of matters of her own heart, Satine was still feeling frustrated that Lukas and she were forever running into each other for only brief snatches of time. She resolved to try and do something about sorting a specific time to spend with him once they had some definite news on how Mixed Emotions was going to shape up.

Not a natural cook by any means, Ava was undoubtedly a fine host. The large dining table in the corner of the lounge area had been decorated beautifully for the evening. The cuisine itself had largely been left to Satine. This suited both women, as Satine had enjoyed actually having the space to put some of her mother's recipes into action. It also meant that she could spend that week's phone call home asking Iodine for updated tips on how to go about preparing her menu. She needed no such reminder, naturally, as all of her mother's recipes were imprinted on her heart. However, it meant that the conversation could be filled with Iodine patiently and joyously recounting all of her cooking tips and left no time to discuss the issue of the absent progress with Mixed Emotions.

Claude arrived on the dot of the allocated time of 7pm, clutching several bottles of wine and a large bunch of flowers. He set up position on one of the stools at the breakfast bar as Satine poured wine and put the last touches to the various pots of delicious-smelling fayre that bubbled away on the gas hob. Ava arranged the flowers into a centre-piece for the table and they chatted amiably until Cicely arrived about fifteen minutes later. Cicely wore a billowing cream kaftan and her hair was wrapped in a matching turban, topped off with a diamond and gold clip that sported a bright feather. She looked radiant and every inch the star – a fact that did not fail to both impress and also alarm the other members of Mixed Emotions. She came with armfuls of wine bottles and a box of very expensive looking chocolates. To everyone's relief, the conversation flowed naturally – starting unsurprisingly with a joint moan about the club and their frustrations about getting nowhere fast with Rosie. The fact that they shared the same negative view of the song they had been given to perform was another hot topic, although Satine was keen to pass on the assurance that Lukas had given them that the end result would pleasantly surprise them all. As she said this, she could not help but notice that she felt self-conscious even mentioning Lukas's name to the group and resolved further that she would be pro-active in trying to organise a date with him as soon as it seemed possible. Now that Cicely had been drawn out in her negative comments about Rosie, the others felt comfortable in sharing their growing dislike.

'She seems to like you more than us – she certainly talks to you more at the club. Can you work on pumping her for more info?' Satine asked Cicely.

'I told you that she knows nothing more than the drips of information S.K. gives her, despite the fact that she acts like she knows everything. As soon as she has news of any kind, she won't hesitate to let us all know. She gets off on the idea of having all the answers, even if she doesn't know anything,' Cicely reassured her as Ava carried the first of their courses to the table. Each course was a triumph and Satine basked in the appreciative comments of Claude, Cicely and Ava. She noticed that Ava did not eat a great deal herself, but she knew that she was preoccupied with thoughts of Glen despite the very good job she was doing of being the consummate host. The dinner table chat was light for the rest of the courses, but as the wine flowed the inevitable delving into affairs of the heart started to emerge.

'Any progress with lovely Lukas – he of the nice smile and even nicer bum! And I don't mean just the business talk you've already told us about!' Claude smiled cheekily as he downed the remains of his third glass of wine and helped himself to another. Satine flushed slightly, but had already had two glasses herself and was not feeling all that bashful anymore when she thought about it:

'Well, chance would be a very fine thing! I hardly see him. For all I know, he might not even be single.'

'He's single – and he likes you! Not that you didn't know the last part.' Claude winked at her and she was a little shocked at how happy his words had made her feel. Ever protective of Satine, Ava jumped in to quiz Claude a little more:

'How do you know he's single?'

'S.K. and Rosie have me delivering things back and forth to the studio all the time. Lukas and I talk a little.' Claude paused, remembering wistfully that he had been quite taken with Lukas himself and their early chats were full of hopefulness for Claude. However, it was immediately obvious that, although extremely comfortable with Claude's sexuality, Lukas was definitely interested in women – and Satine, in particular. 'He talks about Satine all the time. He pretends to be interested in hearing about Ava too, but he brings the subject back to Miss Smitten over there all the time.' He blew Satine a little kiss and she blushed with excitement at hearing the words.

'I could be offended at that,' Ava joked.

'I think you have more than enough male attention from that handsome young man – Glen?' This was from Cicely. She had been drinking a little more slowly and carefully than the others, but even she was now on her second very large glass of red wine.

'Not this week,' Ava frowned, 'but yes – things are going well.'

'Good for you! Now,' Cicely turned her attention to Satine, ' I think we need to give fate a little push in the right direction with you and Lukas. I will tell Rosie you need a weekend night off from the club and I will make sure Lukas is free too.'

'You have that power?' This was from Claude.

'Let's just say, I can talk her round. A happy band makes for a successful business.' She smiled at Satine, looking directly into her eyes in a manner that was as unguarded as it was friendly. Although pleasant, there had always been that slight disconnection on the rare occasions when they had talked before this evening. 'Leave it to me.' Cicely surprised Satine even more by reaching across the table and patting the top of her hand. Ava found herself smiling at the thought of Glen and how right he had been about the dinner party. Clever and gorgeous.

At that precise moment, as the Mixed Emotions laughed and bonded over dinner, Cooper was in the same phone booth as usual – holding the receiver away from his ear as Dakin ranted.

'So far, I'd call it a fat lot of nothing you've given me! Accounts are breathing down my neck again about how much you are costing the department.'

'Not much where accommodation is concerned, I can assure you! I'm getting sick of that dingy rat hole! A self-respecting dingo wouldn't sleep in it!' Cooper was tiring of being so placatory with Dakin. To his surprise, Dakin seemed to have burnt out his aggression and his tone became more moderate:

'Well, the German version of the fucking Ritz was fully booked! Just get something on her that we can use. And get it quickly!'

'Any day now -any day!' Cooper was not sure if Dakin had put the phone down before he had finished speaking or immediately after.

Later, Claude excused himself from the party saying that he was meeting someone in a club in the town centre. When grilled, he became coy and said he would let them know how it went if there was anything to report. After he had gone, the three women took up positions on the sofas and sipped at coffees that they hoped would mop up some of the copious amounts of wine they had consumed.

'He didn't seem drunk at all!' Cicely marvelled at the energetic way in which Claude had bounced out of the apartment after kissing them all telling them what a blast he had had in their company.

'That's what growing up in France will do for you!' Ava replied.' He's used to wine.' She winced a little, her fuzzy head reminding her that she was not so used to the grape.

'He's such a sweet boy. I hope he's alright.' Cicely smiled sadly. 'There is a lot of hatred out there. I hope he is careful.'

'I worry about him too,' Ava confessed, 'but he's no fool and I think he can take care of himself.'

'I hope he finds someone to take care of him too.' Cicely seemed to look far into the distance, as if suddenly recalling something that made the smile fade. Noticing this, Satine asked her:

'Anybody special for you?' It was blunt; Satine realised that as soon as she said the words but the wine had loosened both her tongue and her judgement. To her relief, the smile came back to Cicely's face and she replied:

'Not at the moment. I think I am happier on my own.' Again there was that phasing out in her eyes, Satine noticed, as if Cicely kept being transported to another time and another place. Whatever the memory was, Satine could tell that it was not a happy one. Cicely drained her coffee cup a few moments later and announced that she should go as she was feeling tired. Sleepy themselves, Satine and Ava called her a taxi and waved her off a few minutes later.

As Ava fell into a contented slumber, she thought how pleased Glen would be when she told him his idea had been a great one – Mixed Emotions were bonding beautifully.

Cooper decided to call in at the club to 'surprise' Ava the following night. He could hardly supress his delight when he saw Ava standing with Cicely at the end of the bar nearest the staircase as he arrived. The two looked like they were having quite an animated chat which made Cooper congratulate himself once again. He noticed that there was another, extremely attractive woman standing with the two.

'Surprise!' Cooper shouted as he walked towards Ava. Her face lit up as he expected and they hugged.

'He's even more handsome than you said!' The attractive stranger cooed as he broke free of his embrace. Ava quickly introduced the woman as Tamara. He smiled broadly as he shook her hand, partly at the compliment Tamara had given but also at the confirmation that Ava was smitten. Tamara excused herself, saying that she had to prepare herself for the 'first show.' Cooper watched as she walked off towards a door marked 'staff only', admiring her figure as she departed. He made a mental note to make sure that he has an unrestricted view of the podiums at show time. He turned his attention to Cicely:

'And you *must* be Cicely!' Cooper beamed at her, but immediately regretted what he had said as Cicely arched her eyebrow and gave him a very cold look. Cooper cursed himself for making such a silly error, no doubt the result of being distracted by Tamara's beauty and the thought of the forthcoming show.

'Must I?' Cicely replied, her expression remaining fixed and steely.

'Well...I guessed. Ava talks about Mixed Emotions all the time, of course! I've met Satine, and I was pretty sure you couldn't be Claude!' Not great, thought Cooper, but not a bad save either. Cicely continued to look coldly for a few moments more, but seemed to decide that there was no harm done.

'Yes, I'm Cicely.' She added nothing further, but smiled slightly as she spoke. There was no warmth in her tone, Cooper noted. 'Well, I had better leave you two lovebirds in peace. Rosie has started giving me one of her looks, so I guess I'm needed.' With this, she turned and headed off towards the far side of the bar where Rosie stood.

'Not sure she likes me.' Cooper gave Ava a playful wince as he spoke.

'Oh, she's just a bit cool at first – like I said. But last night really did pay off! It was a great idea.' Ava squeezed his hand. 'Thank you. Cicely was much more relaxed and open.'

And I nearly derailed things by spooking her out, thought Cooper. He resolved there and then that he would have to take himself out of the way where Cicely was concerned and rely on Ava to find her way to the information her needed. The work on the signalling systems would just have to take him 'out of town' quite a bit in the near future. Dakin would be a pain, but clearly it was a mistake to underestimate Cicely's caution around strangers. It was also clear to Cooper that she really was a woman with something to hide and Dakin's obsession made more sense now. He gave Ava a peck on the cheek, saying that he could only stay for half an hour as he had a very early start. She was delighted that he had made the effort, so the decision to drop by at the club had not been a disaster. As a reward, Cooper very much hoped that Tamara would be taking her clothes off soon.

That Saturday night saw the club busier than Satine and Ava had ever experienced. Cicely had been drafted in at the last minute by Rosie and the ranks of new strippers had been swelled. Lotte and Tamara still had the key spots, but the dances were performed with more regularity as the streams of men arriving continued late into the evening. Many of them were a lot younger and fitter than Ava and Satine were used to – almost as if a naval cruiser had docked and released its marines for a night on the town. Even their 'guests' during the evening seemed more alert and they had barely risked the usual champagne spilling. Comparing notes with Cicely when they coincided in the bathroom, Satine soon learned that her companion had been experiencing the same with the two men who had joined her for drinks. Cicely shrugged it off as being 'just one of those nights' and was cheered at the prospect that Rosie would not be raking in much from either of them that night. Not that it would concern Rosie, considering the amount of cash that was raining down on the strippers as they performed. The dance floor around the podiums was crammed with very energetic man, none of which were staggering or seeming worse for wear. Mr Dead and a few of the more familiar faces formed a tight circle near the bar area, with Rosie flitting about amongst them to ensure that they were not too put out by the influx of the new crowd. It certainly changed the dynamic of the club and the air was charged with something that Rosie did not like. Her displeasure manifested by making her shrieking laughter more forced and unconvincing than usual.

At 1am precisely, Ava had just returned from the bathroom when the music was abruptly silenced. The full lights of the club flicked on at the same time and she winced at the brightness. Before she could adjust to the glare, she found herself being pushed into the nearest wall, her face shoved roughly against it. She gasped, confused and angry. Whoever had pushed her was still holding onto her arms, forcing them together so that her chest was painfully expanded. She cried out, convinced that the ubiquitous security staff would be on her attacker at any second. Violence against the women in the club was very rare, but always dealt with immediately. But nobody came. She became aware that her wrists were being pushed together, and seconds later cold steel wrapped around them. She was being handcuffed. She became aware of a deep, male voice speaking German in her ear. She was being arrested and read her rights! She twisted her face so that she could see across the club and, still blinking into the brightness, she could see a mass of hectic movement all around.

As Ava watched, she could see that many of the young 'customers' had pulled out police badges and were cuffing any of the club staff that were near them. Already, there were about six handcuffed figures being corralled onto the now empty dance floor and told to sit and stay silent. Ava noticed that Tamara and Lotte were amongst them. Panicking, she looked across to where Satine had been sitting in their usual booth. To her horror, she saw Satine being pushed roughly towards the group on the dance floor, her hands behind her back and the same look of panic in her face that mirrored the other women. The 'customers' were being joined by more officers, this time in uniform. About a dozen of them surged up the stairway, immediately replicating the actions of their plain-clothed fellows and arresting anyone that they came upon.

Ava was pushed towards the gathering area on the dance floor. Looking over her shoulder, she saw that both Cicely and Rosie were being herded along too. The latter was shrieking in German and struggling against the two officers that had hold of her arms. Cicely was silent, her face frozen and her eyes cast downwards.

Ava found herself kneeling next to Satine when she reached the dance floor. The two women pushed their shoulders together – the only form of reassuring bodily contact that the handcuffs permitted them to express.

'What the hell is happening?!' Satine hissed.

'A raid! We should have known all these men were police. It seems obvious now!' Someone behind them barked in German – an order to stop talking, no doubt. The two women complied, pushing their shoulders tightly together again in a futile attempt at comfort. Across the dance floor that was now becoming a makeshift transit camp, Tamara and Lotte were facing them. Fortunately for them, the raid had started after one of their dances had ended so they were clad in towelling robes. A new dancer beside Lotte was not so fortunate as was wearing nothing but the silver bikini and feather boa she had been performing in just minutes earlier. Lotte's face was a mask of spite and she was yelling in German at two of the police men but they took no notice of her at all. Tamara was sobbing silently, crumpled and dejected. They became aware that Rosie was now just behind them. Cicely knelt beside Ava but Rosie clearly had no intentions of complying. As they watched, two young officers abandoned their attempts to quieten Rosie and shouted across the bar area. In an instant, a giant of a man with a bald head and a lantern jaw turned towards them. They noticed that the man was talking to Mr Dead but, at the call of the officers, he curtailed his conversation and marched across the room to them. The two officers whispered something to him and, as he listened, the man glared unblinking at Rosie. He began talking to Rosie in German. His voice was deep and he did not raise it at all. However, the effect on Rosie was immediate and distinct: Rosie nodded after the man had spoken and, without a word, took up a kneeling position on the dance floor next to Cicely.

'Who is that man?' Cicely hissed out of the corner of her mouth.

'Chief Inspector Hans Gruber.' Rosie said the name like it should mean something to Cicely and the others. She observed the blank looks that Cicely, Ava and Satine returned and sighed:

'He's pretty much the law in Hanover. If he has sanctioned this raid, we had all better keep our mouths shut and pray he is just making a point.'

'What do you mean, 'making a point'?' Satine whispered.

'Gruber does this now and again – usually just to show everyone he can do what he likes. He hasn't picked on us before, but every six months or so some club gets the treatment.'

'What are they looking for?' Ava asked.

'Evidence of money laundering – which they won't find!' Rosie said this with an attempt at sounding smug, but the women could see by her trembling bottom lip that she was scared. 'They will also look for drugs – which they also will not find. We are clean.' None of the women knew precisely how to take this last statement. Certainly, none of them had seen any evidence of illegal drug use or sales in the club but Rosie's use of the word 'clean' could have meant that tracks were always well covered.

'You don't think that some of our 'guests' have reported us for rinsing them?' Satine articulated what the other women were thinking. They had become used to their activities and seldom thought much about it now, but it was immoral and probably even a specifically named crime. In response, Rosie looked scornful and her eyes flitted between the others as she spoke:

'We do nothing here that isn't happening elsewhere. You just keep your heads and tell them nothing if they ask. You are singers in S.K.'s new band, hanging out here with me.

Got it?' She gave each of them in turn a hard stare until they had all nodded their agreement.

Rosie's use of the words 'if they ask' had given Satine, Ava and Cicely a false sense of relief as they all started to entertain the fantasy that the raid would be over and done with after Gruber's men had searched for drugs. This was quickly extinguished when the officers began to take the occupants of the dance floor out of the club one by one. Rosie was taken first, her head down and silent in a complete reversal of how she had been conducted to the dance floor. Satine found herself the last to be taken out, marching just a few paces behind the distraught Tamara.

When she hit the cold night air, Satine was dazzled by the array of police cars and two large, windowless vans. The first of the vans pulled away from the kerb as she watched and she was then lined up to get into the remaining transporter. Once inside, she found that the sparse interior consisted of two rows of benches that faced each other. She took up the last space on the left side row, sitting opposite Tamara. She tried to nod silent reassurances to Tamara, but the dancer's eyes were fixed on the floor. Seconds later, one of the two officers who were standing in the aisle of the van pulled the heavy doors of the rear of it shut. Satine was nearly thrown into the aisle as the van roared away from the kerb. The mercifully short journey was bumpy and silent. As she scanned the rest of the seated occupants, Satine was alarmed that she only really recognised Tamara and Lotte. The rest of the ten occupants were all the new dancers and bar staff that had been taken on since she and Ava had arrived. Cicely, Ava and Rosie must all be in the other van, Satine realised with a shiver. Even Rosie's presence would have made her feel a little less scared. The image of her mother filled her mind and she felt a sickening drop in her stomach at the thought of Iodine finding out that she was currently handcuffed and surrounded by strippers on their way to the local jail.

As the police vans were speeding their way to the imposing central headquarters, Glen Cooper was anxiously urging a taxi driver to get him to the same building as quickly as possible. He had been fast asleep when the night porter at the hotel had knocked imploringly on his door, saying that there had been an urgent telegram. Blearily, Cooper had read the short communication and hastily dressed. He found himself waiting outside the usual phone booth in the dark as a howling gale whipped at his face until all traces of sleep were blasted away. The phone rang after he had been there about five minutes and he snatched it up after the first ring:

'Cooper.'

'The shit's about to hit the fan big style.' Dakin's voice sounded even more aggressive than ever, if that were actually possible. Cooper wondered if those stories of spontaneous human combustion were actually true and, if so, how long before some poor office cleaner found Dakin spread up the walls?

'What-'

'No talking. Just listen. We got word that some arsehole Chief of Police called Gruber has decided that Klub Kasbah is to be this month's showcase raid recipient. This prick seems to think it makes him look the part if he turns over somewhere without warning every so often. Sends the right kind of signal out, apparently.'

'Oh, shit! When?'

'About an hour ago.'

'How did you know?'

'I've got a contact in the mayor's office there….and everywhere else, of course. Gruber had to get it signed off first. I'm about to speak to the turd the minute he gets back from the raid.' Cooper could not help but be impressed that, incandescent with rage though he was, Dakin had managed to vary his vocabulary about Gruber. He had been an arsehole, a prick and now a turd. What next, Cooper wondered. He soon got his answer:

'Get over there and make sure that this just all goes away. You might need to give the wanker something so he can keep face. Vain as they come, by all accounts.'

'Like what?'

'You'll think of something. And make it good.' The phone line clicked off.

Satine was 'processed' first when the van reached its destination as she was nearest the door as they were taken out. Processing involved two stony-faced female officers roughly patting her down and barking at her to put her possessions on a plastic tray. It was only then that she realised that she had left her handbag in the club. She told the two officers this, trying to use as many German words as she could in the hope that her cooperation would work in her favour. Unimpressed, the dour women merely shoved the empty tray aside and escorted Satine along a grey, featureless corridor and then into a small cell. The door

178

was slammed behind her and she heard the terrifying clunk of the bolt being sunk. The room was bare except for a small toilet bowl with no seat, a little metal sink and a narrow bench with a thin mattress covered in a blue plastic shell. She sat on the corner of the mattress feeling as alone and terrified as she could ever imagine.

Her relief was overwhelming when, about five minutes later, the door was opened again and Lotte and one of the new girls were placed inside the cell. The girl was another of the unlucky ones who had been nearly naked when the raid started. Evidently, one of the officers had taken pity on her and she was wrapped in a red blanket that at least covered her torso adequately. However, her bare legs looked blue with cold and one of the heels of her shoes was broken off, causing her to limp awkwardly.

'Guess they're packing us in tonight! The bastards!' Lotte shouted the last two words at the door in the hope that the two surly women would hear her insult. Satine could not help but admire the was that Lotte seemed totally undiminished by what was going on around them. The unfamiliar dancer looked wide-eyed and fearful and Satine tried to give her a weak smile. In response, the young girl just pushed past Lotte and slumped on the mattress, leaning her head against the cold wall and shutting her eyes. Fair enough, thought Satine.

'They haven't even given us our phone call!' Lotte ranted as she sat next to Satine. 'This is all bullshit!'

'Where's Tamara?'

'She threw up when they searched her. They had to take her to the bathroom to clean up. Hope she puked on them!' Lotte shouted this again at the locked door.

Tamara had, alas, only managed to be sick on herself. One of the grim female officers had watched her as she washed herself and sponged at the stain on her robe with wet toilet paper. The female officer showed her impatience by rapping her fingers against the roller towel housing on the wall and Tamara quickly rinsed her tear-stained face in cold water. Moments later, she was being taken along the long corridor towards the holding cells. Ahead of her, she could see three of the club workers that had been in the van with filing into a cell. As they were locked in, she looked further along the corridor to where it branched out into a small reception area. A low counter ran the length of it and two uniformed officers were both seated at it. One of them was talking to another figure who stood leaning on the counter. The figure was a tall and very handsome male.

He was speaking intently to the seated officer and there was no mistaking the anger in his face. She could not hear what he was actually saying, but it was clear that the desk sergeant was being berated in the strongest manner by the young man. As she watched, the man looked up and in her direction. Tamara froze as she realised that she recognised him! It was the Australian man that Ava had started dating, Tamara was sure of it. Glen Cooper. The man looked back at her and a flash of panic washed over his face as he realised that she was looking at him with recognition. He quickly turned away. Realising that she had stopped moving, Tamara's escorting officer gave her a sharp push on the shoulder and she was moved along. The officer opened the door to the last cell on the corridor which was only about five metres away from where Ava's boyfriend stood. As she was compelled inside, Tamara just caught sight of a new arrival in the reception area walking over to Ava's man and shaking his hand. The new arrival was the bald, angry-looking man who had been obviously in charge during the raid at the club. The cell door was closed on her before Tamara could see anything else.

Cooper noted that the dancer from Ava's club had been put in the cell nearest to the reception area and made a mental note of the number on the door as he spoke to Gruber. The

Chief of Police was clearly in a placatory mood and Cooper was very swiftly led to Gruber's office. Gruber sat at his desk and motioned for Cooper to take a seat in the chair on the opposite side. Cooper noticed that the room was clinical and neat with no traces of personal items anywhere. Used to dirty, nicotine stained and tobacco-filled offices, Cooper was increasingly surprised by the reality of Gruber. He could smell sandalwood soap and an undercurrent of carbolic on the man and Cooper noticed that, although huge shovels with thick black hair snaking up from the wrists, Gruber's hands were clean and immaculately manicured. This was a man who did not plan on stopping at his current title, Cooper realised. Gruber was groomed and ready for even better things, political office perhaps. The crisp white shirt he wore was starched and pristine, showing no sign of the hectic activity of his night's work. The groomed exterior was only really belied by the flat and bent nose that had clearly been broken on more than one occasion. Gruber looked at Cooper with eyes that seemed to be trying to supress rage. No wonder, thought Cooper – Gruber was not used to having anyone rain on his parade. Cooper could only imagine the demeanour with which Dakin had approached the Chief of Police. However, Cooper was confident that Gruber would keep his anger in check until he had departed. After that, Cooper was sure that every junior officer in the building would be on the receiving end of Gruber's ire. But, for now, things would be played very nicely.

'So, your Mr Dakin has explained that tonight's action may be....contrary to international interests.' Gruber's English was flawless, Cooper noted. 'But.....such an expensive use of resources cannot be seen to be squandered. The tax payers will not take kindly to it, and neither will the mayor.' Cooper nodded, more as an inner confirmation to himself that Gruber was as ambitious and politically minded as he had guessed than in agreement with the man's words.

'Mr Dakin is aware of that,' Cooper leaned forward. ' And I am sure that you will find a few of the ladies you have in your cells currently do not have all the necessary papers to justify their stay in your country. Make an example of a few of them, by all means. Just make sure that the people we need to walk out of here can do so quickly and without any fuss.'

'And they would be whom?' Gruber betrayed nothing in the tone of his voice, but Dakin knew that he would be eager to salvage as much as he could from the raid.

'I will give you a list. The owner's wife and some of her circle, essentially. They get to walk out immediately, most of the others can have a night in the cells and then send them home too. Now,' Cooper knew that his next words would have to nail the 'something' that Dakin needed him to think up. 'I take it that deporting a few illegals won't cut it as justification for tonight's costly little enterprise?'

'Hardly. I'm supposed to be winning the war on organised crime and drug dealing.'

'Well, how would it be if you had it from a reliable source that there was a large amount of cocaine being stored in the grotty little flat of one of the strippers? A tip off that was reliable enough to warrant a search whilst the little tart was banged up in here for the night?' Cooper leaned back and grinned at Gruber.

'And that person would be…?' Gruber was beginning to smile broadly too. A decent drug bust would do the trick perfectly, regardless of where the drugs actually came from, and it seemed that this Australian would ensure that Dakin would make the magic happen.

Cooper gave Gruber a description of Tamara and the number of the cell that he had seen her put inside.

He had, indeed, thought of something.

Within the hour, Rosie, Ava, Satine and Cicely were standing outside the police headquarters in a bemused state. They had been taken from their respective cells without any explanation, leaving their cell mates to protests pointlessly as the doors were slammed shut on them again. Once gathered in the reception area, a tired desk officer had announced that they were free to go and asked if they needed to make a phone call to arrange transport. Rosie had used the telephone she was directed to and returned minutes later to the others. She had simply said that 'it was in hand' and made her way outside. The others followed.

'What about Lotte, Tam and the others? Why have they been kept in the cells?' Satine had demanded. In response, Rosie just shrugged and snarled that she should just be grateful that the ordeal was over for her and that S.K. would 'deal with everything.' Cicely, Ava and Satine had started to protest, but Rosie just lit a cigarette and turned her back to them.

Minutes later, the longest and widest car Satine and Ava had ever seen slid into view and came to a halt at the kerb right beside them. It was a limousine, but of a type that they did not imagine could actually exist outside of a

Hollywood movie. The car was jet black, the windows tinted like huge sunglasses. A uniformed driver emerged, complete with a peaked cap. He scurried round to one of the rear passenger doors and opened it. Mr Dead emerged and instantly took both of Rosie's hands in his, mumbling reassurances. He turned to Satine and the others and said:

'Miss Satine. Ladies. Please, let me escort you away from this horrible place.'

Stunned into silence, the women followed Rosie into the vehicle. The interior was as sumptuous as the exterior, with red velvet trim and black leather seats. It escaped none of them that the interior bore more than a passing resemblance to a very plush coffin.

'Have we actually died? Is this our ride to heaven?' Ava whispered to the others as the car began to move.

'Doubt it,' replied Cicely. 'Unless they are planning on dropping Rosie off in Hell first!' The three began to snigger and this soon turned into hysteria – relief more than mirth taking over the women in the wake of the night's drama and terror. Rosie shot them evil looks, but this only made them cackle more.

'Are you all out of your minds?!' Rosie spat.

'Leave them, Miss Rosie,' Mr Dead purred, patting Rosie's hand. 'They have had a terrible shock. I think they need to release things as best they can.' Rosie smiled tightly, but her eyes still shot venom at the other women. Again, this only made them laugh even harder still. However, as the laughter eventually subsided, both Satine and Ava realised that they had actually started to weep. They fell into each other's arms as a wave of sorrow hit them. Cicely seemed on the brink of tears too, but was clearly holding herself back. She turned her face away from the others and stared out into the night.

Mr Dead had insisted that the women all came for a much needed drink at his home before they were taken to their own places. The mansion of the Stiefel dynasty was every bit as palatial in size and gothic grandeur as Satine had been expecting. However, there was also a somewhat abandoned, neglected and faded aspect to the grounds and the exterior of the building. Even in the moonlight, the faded and cracked stucco was evident in many places and ivy pushed its way into window frames here and there too. They climbed out of the limo by a huge fountain that stood proudly on a circular piece of lawn that served as an island for vehicles to sweep up to the grand entrance and depart. The fountain featured an array of stone seahorses, pulling a barnacle encrusted chariot. Trident waving and hair flowing, Poseidon stood at the bow and glowered down at new arrivals. Lit from beneath the surface, jets of water cascaded up and down to give a sense that the seahorses were galloping through the waves.

They were led by Mr Dead into a vast ante hall. In the centre of it, a huge curved staircase disappeared up into the darkness. Satine could imagine a deranged Norma Desmond stalking down the stairs with her mad eyes imploring for applause. Mr Dead ushered them to a door to the left of the stairs and they found themselves in a grand sitting room. A sumptuous, white marble fireplace occupied one room, a crackling fire radiating cloying heat and casting the softly lit room in an orange glow. Above the fireplace, a shy and awkward figure looked down at them. He had a halo of unruly curls that framed the chubby, kind face. The face itself was partially in shadow, and Satine recognised it immediately as one of the many self-portraits painted by Rembrandt. The partially obscured face, Satine remembered reading, was the Dutch Master's way of conveying his insecurity as a young painter. Satine had absolutely no doubt that the painting was an original and could only guess at its value.

Once seated on beautiful French salon furniture, Mr Dead poured them all large glasses of brandy from a cut-glass decanter that sat on a silver tray on a small table by the fireplace. The warmth of the room and the soothing brandy soon calmed the women and they fell into a contented silence.

This silence was broken after a few minutes by a shrill cry from the darkness above the staircase. They heard a woman's voice demanding in German and repeated cries of 'Hans?' being shouted in the darkness.

All eyes in the room turned to the blackened recesses of the staircase. Seconds later, a figure emerged from the darkness and began descending towards them. Satine blinked at the figure, convinced for a moment that the mythic Norma Desmond had indeed emerged. Although only about four and a half feet tall, the figure seemed much bigger and cast a shadow on the wall like a huge spider. She was wrapped in a night robe of red satin that billowed as she moved; her head was wrapped in a matching turban, the face beneath it a ghastly white mask. The woman swept from the bottom stair and across the floor to stand in the centre of the room.

Mr Dead and the woman exchanged a few words in German. The woman nodded and her eyes swept the room, taking in each of the women with cool and supremely unabashed stares. When her eyes fell on Rosie, she smiled in recognition.

'Frau Shultz-Klopper!' The two exchanged pleasantries, after which she turned back to Mr Dead with further questions. The two conversed hastily for a few moments, before Mr Dead addressed Satine, Ava and Cicely:

'Allow me to introduce my mother, Frau Hildegard Stiefel. Mother, these ladies are singers in the Shultz-Klopper's latest pop group. I told you all about it.' Speaking English for the benefit of his guests did not result in his mother following suit. She rasped something at her son, clearly unpleasant. As she spoke, she eyed Satine, Ava and Cicely coldly. Moments later, she swept out of the room and ascended the stairs back into the darkness from which she had emerged. Mr Dead looked embarrassed.

'My mother was disturbed by our arrival. She does not sleep well. Forgive me, ' Mr Dead began to follow his mother. 'I will be back in a moment. Please – have more brandy.'

'What did she say?' Satine asked Rosie as soon as he had departed.

'She said you looked more like whores than singers.' Rosie replied flatly.

After the translation of Hildegard Stiefel's words, the women fully expected that Mr Dead had gone to summon his driver and that they would soon be ejected from the mansion. However, about ten minutes later mother and son re-appeared. Hildegard Stiefel was now clad in a pair of beige slacks and a black turtleneck sweater. The turban had been replaced by an expensive but still obvious blonde wig with corkscrew curls. She had applied a dark red lipstick and the air was filled with the unmistakable scent of Chanel No 5 as she swept into the sitting room.

'Please forgive my rudeness!' She purred in perfect English. 'It is the early hours of the morning, after all!' She poured herself a brandy and extracted a cigarette from a silver box on the table. She waited for Mr Dead to light it for her, which he did immediately and wordlessly. She took a deep drag of the cigarette and then continued:

'What a terrible ordeal you must have gone through this evening! Outrageous!'

'Thank you, Frau Stiefel,' Rosie replied with a fawning tone. 'S.K. and I run a very respectable business at the club. We will be complaining to the highest authority about it.'

'Gruber is an opportunistic little runt.' Hildegard said. 'He thinks he is impressing the mayor, but I know differently. We will make sure that this… goes away.' Satine, Ava and Cicely realised that the wheels within wheels of government were clearly something about which the Stiefel family had some considerable influence. Confirming their conclusion, Rosie continued in her toadying manner:

'Thank you, thank you, Frau Stiefel! S.K. will be so grateful too!'

Mercifully, the others were spared any further displays of Rosie's boot-licking by the sudden arrival of another figure to the sitting room. Before they could see the new arrival as she made her way out of the shadows, the women were hit by a wall of scent that eclipsed Hildegard's perfume. The acrid stench of stale urine was unmistakable and their nostrils burned with the shock of it.

The originator of the smell was a small, very old woman. She was clad in a thick, white night dress that covered her from throat to ankles. She was stooped and bore a walking stick, glasses with lenses that were thick like the bottom of milk bottles and an incongruous, broad-brimmed hat with a single faux rose on its left side. She began growling in German as she hobbled into the room. As she moved past them and towards the fire, the women could see a huge damp patch on the back of the night gown. Worse still, there was a slug trail of small drops of urine in her wake.

'My grandmother – Tante Freda Stiefel.' Mr Dead was clearly embarrassed. To their surprise, the old woman turned to the others and grinned. When she spoke, it was in English, albeit very accented:

'Such an hour to have guests! I wondered what all the shouting was about! Such pretty young women, Hans. Is one of these girls your sweetheart? Mm?' Mr Dead blushed and coughed awkwardly.

'No…no…these ladies are….'

'Oh, Hans!' Tante Freda cut off her grandson's awkward fumbling words with a cackle. 'I know that you are hopeless around women! Too much time spent with corpses, that's his trouble.' She laughed. ' A dear, dear boy – just like his father. But my darling son was only really comfortable with the dead, too!' She shot Hildegard a look that confirmed to Satine and the others that the old woman meant this as an insult to his late son's widow. Hildegard's lips tightened but she said nothing – clearly this was not an unusual occurrence. Satine found herself warming to the old woman immediately. There was something very unpleasant about Hildegard, she was sure. She looked at Mr Dead and felt a fresh pang of sympathy for him. Despite the opulent surroundings, she wondered what freedom or actual joy he had ever experienced. The family business must have been a very gilded cage and Satine suspected that Hildegard would have ruined any relationship her son might have attempted to forge with a woman even if he had been able to conquer his innate shyness. At least the old woman was there to stick the knife into her daughter-in-law. As if reading her mind, the old woman spoke again:

'It is so nice to have beautiful and young women in this old house – even if it is an ungodly hour, Hans!' She lingered on the words 'beautiful' and 'young' to emphasise that Hildegard was not in receipt of either glamour or youth. Looking tartly at Rosie, who she obviously recognised from previous visits, she added:

'And Frau Shultz-Klopper! A familiar, *old* face too!'

The old woman excused herself a few minutes later, leaving the pungent smell of urine as a memento for the others. After about half an hour, a tight-lipped and obviously insulted Rosie announced that they should really all be going home to their beds.

Exhausted beyond belief, neither Ava or Satine could sleep when they eventually found themselves in their own beds. They were too worried about what would happen to the others to give in to the fatigue that gripped every bone in their bodies.

The following day would bring answers to their fears.

One way or the other.

Chapter Eight – Very Mixed Emotions

Whether the Stiefel's really had the influence that Hildegard had indicated or whether the club was actually as clean as Rosie insisted, by the following week it seemed to Satine and Ava that everyone but them was acting like the raid had never even happened. The club itself did not re-open for a few days, but all Rosie would say was that it was getting a 'proper clean'. Again, what that actually meant was debatable too, but Ava had got nothing more when she tried pumping Wieler for information.

One thing was now crystal clear to both women, though: they were in no mood to work another shift at the bar, and they agreed that they would confront Rosie and make it very clear that, if things with Mixed Emotions did not start to happen in earnest, then they would be leaving for England by the end of the month. The raid had upset Ava and Satine in a way that they could not get past. Wieler had clearly been under instructions to pamper them in the wake of the incident, and their fridge and food cupboards were stocked full; the coffee table buckled under the weight of a pile of new magazines; they were even left a pile of cash one morning with a note from Rosie that urged them to go shopping for 'some nice things.' Both agreed to leave the money where it lay for the time being as it was all an obvious bribe, and their patience had now been exhausted. Ava had the added misery that Glen had been out of town on a prolonged training course on another type of signal box, apparently, and she had been forced to settle for two rather brief telephone calls. He had listened with obvious sympathy as she related the tale of the raid at the club and was 'just thanking the stars' that Ava had come to no harm. It was not the same as having him beside her, though. Glen had promised he would make it up to Ava that coming weekend and a beautiful bouquet had arrived with a card that read 'thinking of you, gorgeous girl!'

There had been few callers to the apartment in the wake of the raid. Claude had raced around as soon as he had heard the news, insisting that he would stick by whatever the women decided to do where the Shultz-Kloppers were concerned. Cicely had telephoned and indicated that she was at the point of losing patience too, albeit it in the slightly guarded manner that they had become accustomed to where Cicely was concerned. However, it was the sudden arrival of Lotte a week after the raid that finally brought everything to a head…

Satine was curled on the sofa, trying to distract herself with the German edition of Vogue. Her reading skills were improving steadily where the language was concerned, but she was still at the stage where the majority of the text was puzzling so the activity soon palled. Ava had just emerged from her morning bath when Wieler knocked on their door. Lotte stood behind him with a tear-stained and angry face. Pushing past Wieler, she stalked into the apartment, slumping heavily into an armchair and immediately lit up a cigarette. She began talking in a rapid manner, her voice cracking as she tried to keep the sobs and rage at bay:

'The bastards have deported Tamara. They said that she had been drug dealing! Fucking liars! They found a huge stash of cocaine in her room, they said. I don't believe it! I went to the British Embassy yesterday and they kept me waiting for five hours until some fat toad finally agreed to talk to me. Even then, he wouldn't tell me anything more than she had been charged and was in custody.'

'But that's ridiculous!' Ava was almost in tears herself as she listened. 'Tamara is the sweetest girl! She just wanted to get enough money together for her kids. She wouldn't....would she?' Ava tried to dismiss the sudden thought that it just might have been possible that Tamara had been tempted to make some fast cash. Lotte looked at her with recognition -she had clearly had the same thought at some point. But she soon shook her head vigorously and continued:

'I thought that at first, but I've been going around and around with the idea all night. I just don't believe Tam would do anything so dangerous.'

'No,' Ava said after a few moments silence. 'No. She just wouldn't.'

'What will happen if she's convicted?' Satine asked.

'Prison. No doubt. This is bullshit!' Lotte dragged angrily at her cigarette. A tube of ash about an inch long now hung precariously from the end of it and Satine found herself transfixed by it as it defied gravity and stayed attached to the rest of the burning cigarette. None of them needed to say what they were all thinking: if Tamara was sent to prison, the courts would probably deem her mother to be too old to look after the children and they would go into some sort of hideous care home. The sentence could be long, even for a first offence.

'I knew something was wrong the day after,' Lotte continued. 'Everyone else was released by the end of the morning. I waited for her to come out, but she just didn't. Girls kept walking past me, but none of them was Tam. Then it was quiet; everyone had gone. I thought she might have been sick again, so I went back in and asked the desk officer. He said that everyone who was going to be released that day was already out and that I should count myself lucky and go home.' Lotte took another drag on her cigarette, this time dislodging the tube of ash. It dropped into the ashtray that Satine thrust in its path. Ignoring both the ash and Satine's movement, Lotte continued:

'I knew there was something really wrong. I went back to the club, but it was locked up. So, I went to the recording studio. Rosie and S.K. were there. The bastard wouldn't acknowledge me, as usual, but Rosie started her usual crap about it all being 'a little misunderstanding' and that she was sure Tam would 'be quite fine.' Well,' Lotte ditched the spent cigarette and immediately lit up another. 'I wasn't taking any of that off Rosie! I went straight to Mr. Dead at his funeral parlour and told him what had happened. He's kind of weird, but a decent man, I think.'

'Yes,' Satine nodded, 'we know. Could he help?'

'He said he would make some calls, which he obviously did. A few days ago, he said that I needed to go to the

British Embassy and he gave me the name of someone who would speak to me – that was the toad who kept me waiting! Maurice Jenkins. He said that Tam was being looked after and that there was a solicitor appointed to her case. He said she was better off back in the UK if it came to being…being convicted.' Lotte wiped away a tear as she said the last word. 'This is just bullshit!'

Ava and Satine sat in awed silence after Lotte had finished her tale. The sense of powerlessness was overwhelming, but so too was the distinct feeling that there was something very off-kilter going on. After a while, Satine aired her thoughts and the vigorous nods she received from Ava and Lotte showed that they were all thinking alike:

'Tam has been set up to take the fall here. But…for whom and why?'

'Rosie and S.K.?' Ava pondered. Satine shook her head:

'I just don't see what they would have to gain from that. Any drug conviction associated with the club would just make life harder for them, surely.'

'I agree,' replied Lotte. 'The thought crossed my mind too, but like you said, there is nothing they could gain from it and lots they could lose. No, this is something else.'

'That police chief – Gruber, was it? Could he need something to stick to justify the raid? Mr Dead's mother said he was ambitious.' Satine frowned.

'That has more of a ring of truth about it. But it doesn't help Tamara. I just feel so useless!' Lotte thumped her fist on the arm rest of her chair, nearly dislodging the ashtray that Satine had moved there moments before.

Lotte excused herself soon after, declining an offer of coffee. She said that she had to put Cicely and anyone else who needed to know in the picture that morning in the hope that someone might had information that could be of use. Her visit left Ava and Satine even more dejected and uptight.

Their moods had hardly lightened when Wieler knocked at their door early that afternoon. Satine opened the door and forced a tight smile, telling herself that she knew Wieler had turned out to be one the good guys.

'Rosie has telephoned. She asks that you both be ready in one hour for me to take you to the studio.' He paused, noting without surprise that Satine had bristled at the sound of Rosie's name. He smiled and whispered:

'She says that it is very good news – the best! Please…'
He shrugged, the gesture clearly one of submission.
Deciding that shooting the messenger was unjust, Satine
forced herself to nod her agreement. Wieler went without
another word, leaving Satine to break the news to Ava.
Ava's response that she was glad they would be seeing
Rosie surprised Satine – until Ava added the caveat that, as
she wanted to 'fucking murder somebody' then Rosie
would 'be a more that suitable candidate.'

Neither women decided to make any particular effort that
afternoon in their attire. They wore jeans and T-shirts in a
deliberate show of contempt for any hoops that Rosie might
want them to jump through in the name of PR. Satine had
tied her hair back in a tight plait and neither women had
applied more than a minimum of make-up. The fact that
they applied any at all was purely for their own satisfaction.
Wieler drove them in his usual silence, tactfully turning up
the radio in an attempt to defuse the tension in the air.
Satine and Ava stared blankly out at the rainy Hanover
afternoon as the Mercedes snaked its way through the city.

They arrived at the studio to be greeted by an excited
Rosie. She ushered them into the conference room, where
Cicely and Claude were already ensconced. A huge

magnum of champagne was nestled on a bed of ice in a silver bucket surrounded by fluted glasses. Cicely and Claude gave the women puzzled frowns as they entered – clearly, they had no idea what was going on either. Satine felt a fresh flush of anger at the sight of the champagne. Although she did not think that Rosie was responsible, the thought of celebrating while Tamara languished in jail on bogus but life-crippling charges made her sick to the stomach. In no mood to hold her anger in check, she turned on Rosie and shouted:

'I take it we are not here to toast Tam's release! Do you really think there is anything to celebrate!? I don't!'

Rosie blushed with clear embarrassment, which was satisfyingly rare in itself. She seemed about to launch into a stream of the usual, simpering platitudes and false assurances when an internal door at the far end of the conference room burst open. S.K. stood in the door frame, his bulky torso filling it completely. He had another huge champagne bottle in his hand, and he slid his massive palm up the neck of it released the cork. It ricocheted off the ceiling and landed on the floor as a deafening bang rang in their ears.

'Mixed Emotions!' S.K. boomed. 'The single will hit the shops tomorrow! We are already on the radio playlists that count!'

The band members were so taken aback by the fact that S.K. had delivered his news in English (and perfectly good English at that) that they took a few moments to process what they news actually meant. Claude seemed to register the meaning first and filled the room with a whooping yell that rivalled the volume of the champagne cork's firing. S.K. splashed frothing liquid into and around the flutes.

'Oh my God. Really? Finally?' Ava found her voice.

'Yes, my dears!' Rosie seized her opportunity without hesitation. ' We have heard about poor Tamara. Rest assured, we will help in any way we can. But for today – let us raise our glasses to Mixed Emotions!'

'Mixed Emotions!' S.K. echoed. One by one, the others plucked a glass from the table and raised it. S.K. departed through the door that he had emerged through within ten minutes, not uttering another word in English. This, at least, seemed normal to the others. When Rosie had flittered off after S.K., Cicely confided that Lotte had informed her of the situation with Tamara.

'I have no doubt that she has been set up. You can't trust…' she let the sentence die in her throat, and Satine wondered what she was about to say. 'You can't trust anyone?' 'You can't trust the police?' Either way, it seemed that Cicely had a very clear and jaundiced view of the authorities. The feeling that there was something more to Cicely than met the eye was never far away for Satine. Claude insisted on being filled in on the story about Tamara and, even though he had not met her, he nodded in his typically sweet and sensitive manner as they informed him.

About half an hour later, Satine was delighted to see Lukas arrive at the studio. He buckled as he carried an enormous cardboard box with him. Setting it down on the conference table, he opened the flap at the top to reveal piles of the newly pressed 45 inch single of Mixed Emotions by Mixed Emotions.

'Ta da!' Lukas grinned. Spontaneously, Satine leaned over and kissed him on the cheek. She froze the second after she had done it, but Lukas grinned all the more and, without hesitation he returned the compliment. However, much to Satine's delighted embarrassment, Lukas kissed her squarely on the lips. Although not much more than a peck, the second where his soft lips toughed hers gave

Satine the sort of tingle that the magazines always said was the sign of 'Mr Right.' They looked at each other for a moment, before an excited Claude pushed between them and plucked one of the 45s from the pile and began to scrutinize the sleeve images. Satine, grinning from ear to ear, took a close look at one of the singles too. The lettering of 'Mixed Emotions' was in white against a blue background at the top of the square. Beneath it was a photograph of the four of them. Cicely was, as expected, central in the composition, but Ava and Satine were still prominent at each side of her, with Claude crouched in the foreground. All four of them looked great, Satine thought. She looked up briefly as she turned the disc over, and was delighted to see that Lukas was looking at her with the same beautiful, dimpled smile.

'Can I take you to dinner tonight?' he asked.

'Yes, please.' Satine replied in such a simple but heartfelt manner. A day that had begun so horribly had, in an instant, been transformed into something beautiful.

It all went straight back to horror as she looked at the images on the back of the disc!

The back cover of the sleeve consisted of black central lozenge, over which white lettering gave the usual writing and production credits. Around this information were a series of montage shots of the band. There was a shot of Cicely on her own which, although a little irksome, was not a particular surprise considering how much of the lead vocals she had been given and the obvious bias Rosie had always shown. However, a panel on the opposite side had an image of just Satine and Ava, so that balanced out Satine's reaction immediately. An image of Claude standing was also featured, with a small image of the whole band in the bottom left corner. It was this image that made Satine's stomach drop like a stone: clustered on the dance floor was a smiling Cicely, a pouting Claude, a smouldering Ava....and Candy the hooker!

'Oh my God!' For a moment, Satine thought the words were hers, but she quickly realised that Ava had shouted out. Turning, Satine saw that Ava was scrutinising the same image. One by one, everyone in the room fell into awed silence as they saw Candy's face looking sullenly up at them from the sleeve of the 45.

'Oh! They have arrived! It's so exciting – yes?' With impeccable timing, Rosie bounced back into the room.

'Thrilling!' Satine snarled. Without another word, she thrust the record she was holding into Rosie's chest and marched out of the room. Ava went to follow, but Lukas caught her by the shoulder and asked if he could go instead. Ava fought back her protective instinct and nodded.

Satine slumped against the wall of the studio, oblivious to the cold wind that had started to build as the afternoon drew dim. She tried to calm her breathing with little success, her head pounding and a confusion of thoughts galloping through her mind.

'Don't let it spoil things,' Lukas stood beside her, inclining his head towards her so that it rested against her shoulder. It felt good, and Satine exhaled deeply. 'It was all put together in a rush. S.K. and Rosie must have known you would be ready to walk after the raid.'

'We were! We honestly were. And when Lotte told us about Tam I thought…well,' Satine was still mindful of remembering to breathe as she spoke, 'well, we were both ready to go back home.'

'I am really glad you are here.' Lukas said this so softly but with such conviction that Satine found she could do nothing else but kiss him again. This time they fell into each other's arms, kissing passionately and without any awkwardness. They became lost in each other, ignoring the rain that started to lash at them for several minutes until, finally, Lukas broke away from the embrace:

'We'd better get inside before we freeze!' Satine allowed him to take her by both hands and lead her back inside.

  Rosie's face was a still flushed with awkwardness as she flustered up to Satine and spouted apologies about the picture of Candy. It would be rectified before the next print run and, as the song was going to be such a massive international hit, there would be millions of copies that did not have the 'little mistake' of the first run. Boldened by her own spin, Rosie had even remarked that the 45 with the wrong picture would probably be an extremely valuable collector's item when Mixed Emotions were superstars.

'If that happens, make sure Candy gets a royalty,' Cicely purred. 'She will be able to cut back on the blow jobs.'

All of them roared with laughter at this – apart from Rosie, of course.

They were conducted to the top floor studio by Rosie, where S.K. sat at his mixing desk like a the pilot of a space craft. The single was played to them several times throughout the course of the early evening. Lukas had been correct – the single sounded wonderful. Cicely's icy intro merged into pulsating disco beat and even the corny lyrics seemed to take on a more meaningful sound. Satine was proud that she was finally hearing the work of Lukas too. Although she could not know how much of the work had been his as opposed to S.K.'s, the overall effect was a tune that she would expect to hear on Radio One back home and something that would fill a dancefloor at any disco. Even Cicely seemed to be a little giddy with excitement as she heard the song.

Rosie allowed them to leave after running through the schedule for the next week. In two days' time they would travel out of town to a larger studio with a bespoke performance space and stage area. They would be recording a film of the song being performed as 'live' although they would all be miming. This would be vital, Rosie said, as the tape of the session could be copied and sent anywhere and everywhere. They would be making personal appearances as much as possible, certainly, but the video of their pristine performance would have a life of its own and be crucial as a marketing tool. According to Rosie, S.K. thought that the video to a song would be as important as the song itself by the 1980s. To that end, all of them were given a cassette tape of the song and ordered to spend the following day making sure that they were word perfect for the recording. And yes, the costumes from the photoshoot would be worn throughout the video to ensure brand identity.

Wieler played the tape over and over in the car on the journey back, announcing with unaccustomed vigour that it 'sounded like a number one' to him. The fact that they had never heard anything coming from the stereo in his apartment that was less than two hundred years old did not serve to endorse his opinion, but both Ava and Satine were pleasantly surprised that he had bothered to say it in the first place.

Satine went through about ten changes of outfit until Ava pointed out that Lukas had seen them in the hideous Mixed Emotions clothes and had still asked Satine out. After this, Satine changed back into the pretty, gypsy dress that she had put on first and tied a little white scarf though the single plait with which she had styled her hair. She wore brown leather boots with a small heel, giving the overall Spanish influence that she liked so much and knew suited her well.

'Looking gorgeous, kiddo!' Ava announced her verdict on the ensemble. 'And, don't worry, I will have an early night and make sure I'm out of the way later.'

'Who says I won't be coming home alone?' Satine blushed slightly before breaking into a broad grin. 'On the other hand, this has taken an awfully long time to finally happen!'

'You do whatever feels right for you,' Ava kissed Satine on the cheek and then slapped her on the rump with the magazine that she was holding. Without further word, she padded off to the bathroom, blowing a kiss at Satine as she went.

The rain was lashing down when Satine's taxi pulled up in front of the little bistro that Lukas had chosen for their date. She darted the few yards from taxi to the restaurant door, but icy rain still managed to sting the back of her neck, and she shivered as she checked herself in the reflection of the glass door. Pleased by what she saw, Satine pushed open the door and entered the bistro. It was a dimly lit and inviting place – tiny with only six tables dotted around. Most were only for two diners, and Lukas sat at the table furthest away from the entrance. Each table had empty wines on them that blazed with red candles. Copious amounts of wax coated the bottles and the bare wooden table tops were scored and pitted. The whole place had an appealingly shabby aspect and the aroma that emanated from the swing doors to the left of where she stood was rich with garlic. A lone waitress smiled at Satine from her position behind the bar. There were no other patrons except Lukas, and he waved and jumped to his feet as soon as he saw Satine. Kissing her lightly, he took her hand and led her to the table, pulling her chair out for her so she could sit.

the 'You look beautiful,' he flashed that dimpled grin again as he took up his seat again. Satine noticed that he was wearing a crisp, pale blue shirt. They top two buttons were open, and she could see a nest of light brown chest hair just where the fabric was parted. His hair was more definitely parted on the left than usual. The Adam Faith look was straying into Robert Redford, much to Satine's pleasure.

'Not so bad yourself,' Satine returned the compliment with as much nonchalance as she could manage but her heart was pounding in her chest as she spoke and the words came out in an uneven and breathy manner. Noticing her nerves, Lukas stretched his hand out across the table and his fingers curled gently around her own.

'Why has this taken us so long?' Lukas asked, staring deep into Satine's eyes. The soft light dilated his pupils so that they were huge and round, framed by his long, pale lashes.

'I guess we have been ships, passing in the night. That and being a little shy when it comes down to it, maybe.'

'Hard to believe that a star of the stage could be bashful. And a pop star now, too!' Lukas teased.

'Personal things are…not so easy to be confident about. Besides, you could have asked me sooner!'

'Maybe I am a little bashful too.' Lukas gave another of his little grins. Satine thought that, if he was pretending to be gauche it was a very endearing act. The waitress was at their table within minutes, talking to Lukas in a manner that made it clear he was a frequent and liked customer. Satine couldn't help thinking that the waitress was a little too friendly with Lukas and then reproached herself for getting jealous. They ordered wine and the waitress left them with menus.

'Is this place a favourite of yours? It's nice.' Satine looked at the menu. 'What do you recommend?'

Lukas took her through a rundown of his favourite choices, which turned out to be nearly everything on the admittedly small menu. Satine felt happy that he had arranged their date at somewhere that was so familiar to him; it seemed like a trusting and intimate gesture. The evening flowed effortlessly with conversation. Lukas prompted Satine for information about where she had been born and her family; all information was listened to with great interest. She had not experienced such attentive and unselfish behavior on many dates she had endured in England. There was something about his manner that seemed disarming and every interested nod or little hum he made as a phatic show of his attention just seemed to make him even cuter.

They were halfway through their main courses before Satine had chance to direct the flow of their conversation towards Lukas. Taking a sip of her recently re-filled wine glass, she asked:

'So…how does Germany compare with Norway?'

'A little warmer, a lot more crowded.' Lukas smiled, clearly enjoying the recollection of home. Satine noticed that his accent seemed to lose some of the usual neutral tone it customarily carried – as if the thought of Norway itself shaved away some of the time he had spent away from his homeland. She was always charmed by the way her mother would also seem to re-acquire her accent when she spoke to relatives on the telephone.

'Did you grow up in the countryside?'

'A place called Asker, which is actually very close to Oslo. It is really a beautiful place -lovely beaches but woodlands too. Lots of hikers come there. I grew up near the Skaugum estate which is where the royal family lived. Asker is very old – the site of the very first church in Norway, in fact. Sorry,' Lukas smiled apologetically, 'I sound like a guidebook.'

'Not at all! You've listened to me waffling on and I want to hear all about you. Asker sounds lovely.' Satine nodded for Lukas to elaborate. The concept of a man apologising for taking charge of a conversation was, again, something that she could not imagine ever hearing in London.

'My parents both worked for the estate. My mother was a gardener – very talented. She passed away when I was twelve.' He paused, looking away for a moment. Satine reached her hand out and rested it on his wrist, provoking an achingly sweet smile from Lukas.

'I'm sorry.'

'Ah, it was a long time ago. My father was wonderful. Still is.'

'My father died when I was young, too. I feel bad sometimes about being so far away from my mum – not that she would ever make me feel bad.'

'My father is the same. He always tells me how busy he is when I phone him, but I think he makes half of it up so that I don't worry about him.' As he spoke, Lukas gently pulled Satine's hand from his wrist and held it. The first silence descended between them, but it was comfortable and seemed an entirely appropriate after the personal details they had both just revealed. Moments later, Lukas raised the subject of how truly vile Rosie was and the two of them cackled through the remains of their meals.

Indeed, the conversation had flowed so easily that Satine did not acknowledge the fact that no other diners had entered the bistro in the whole time they had been there. She only realised this on a final return from the bathroom and noted the pristine arrangement of the other tables and chairs. It was only when Lukas paid their bill that a group of three people came through the door to take up a table. It seemed like fate had blessed them with two hours of space just for them, as if it was somehow making up for the way that they had been thwarted up until now. Even the rain had stopped especially in honour of them when Satine and

Lukas emerged from the bistro. They found that they were holding hands as they walked slowly along the nearly deserted streets. They fell into a comfortable silence and Satine was thrilled when Lukas paused on street corner to turn to her and kiss her again. They became lost in each other, breaking from their embrace only when the rain began to spatter again. Instinctively, Lukas removed his leather jacket and wrapped it around Satine's shoulders. He put his arm around her waist as they began to walk on, heading for a crossing point on the dual carriageway road ahead. The rain began to intensify again, but neither of them paid it any attention and barely quickened their pace. Across the road, a taxi rank beckoned them enticingly. Satine knew that the destination would be her apartment and that Lukas would be staying the night. It needed no discussion.

As they waited for the crossing light to change in their favour, a freezing splash of water rained down on their legs and jerked them back to reality. A car had deliberately swerved into the puddles at the kerbside as it passed them, spraying plumes of oily and iced water onto them in a purposeful act. Stunned, Lukas and Satine could only gape as the car slowed just past them. An angry-faced youth leaned out of the driver's window and shouted something at them before spitting in their direction. The youth's face ducked back inside the car and he sped away without further comment. Lukas hopped into the road, shaking his fist after the car, but Satine quickly pulled him back as an articulated lorry thundered its horn at him as it approached. Satine asked him what the shouted words meant, but Lukas shook his head.

'Tell me,' Satine said softly, looking into Lukas's eyes. He shook his head, but she nodded and repeated her words. Lukas shot another angry look in the direction the car had gone and spoke without looking at Satine:

'He said I should get myself a white woman and not be a traitor to my race! The gutless bastard!' He turned back to Satine. 'I would rather have not told you that.'

'No', Satine took his hand, 'I wanted to know. I forced you to say it.'

Lukas took Satine into his arms and they stood in the rain for several minutes, both trying and failing to erase the last few minute and take themselves back to the blissful haze they had been under as they walked from the bistro.

They travelled back to Satine's apartment in silence, a tacit understanding that there would be only one drop off for the driver. Ava's bedroom door was closed and the apartment was in darkness when they arrived. However, it was clear from the indentation of the furniture and cushions that Ava had bolted to her room when she heard them arriving and the television was still warm to the touch. Satine poured them both large glasses of red wine and she and Lukas curled up on the sofa. As she towel dried her hair, Satine finally spoke:

'I kick myself every time it catches me out, you know? I can forget that it's out there – that people like that are out there. But it always comes back around.' She swirled the red wine around in her glass, gazing at the little waves of crimson that sloshed against the inside of the bowl. 'It always seems to come back to the surface when I'm not expecting it, though.'

'Morons like that exist everywhere. It makes me sick.' Lukas leaned over and stroked a lock of damp hair away from Satine's left eye. He kisses her again, saying: 'He was just jealous that I was with the most beautiful woman in Hanover.'

'Is the right answer!' Satine slid back on the sofa and Lukas climbed over to her, his mouth finding her neck and kissing it lightly. Stealing herself against becoming lost in the wave of tingling excitement that his touch sent through her, Satine slipped from the sofa and stood before him. He looked puzzled for a moment before she smiled and took his hand; Satine led Lukas to her bedroom door and, wordlessly, they disappeared inside.

Chapter Nine – Lights! Camera! Chart Action…?

Ava kept herself discreetly in her room until she heard the sound of the apartment front door softly open from the inside. She heard Satine and Lukas whispering and giggling for a few moments and then the door was closed gently. Already robed and poised, Ava shot out of her bedroom and confronted Satine as she attempted to tiptoe back across the lounge floor.

'Jezebel!' Ava shrieked. 'On the first date!'

Satine blushed and looked at her feet, at which Ava promptly roared laughing, and threw her arms around her friend. She broke the embrace seconds later with a contorted look of mock horror on her face.

'You reek of sin! Get in that bath and cleanse thyself! Harlot!' Satine stuck her tongue out and trotted off in the direction of the bathroom, shouting over her shoulder:

'You're just jealous I got to christen this joint before you and Glen did!'

'He is a gentleman!' Ava declared, before adding 'Unfortunately. And I want all the details!'

Once washed and dressed, Ava and Satine began the process of learning how to mime to the cassette tape recording of their song. It soon became a bore, as their roles were glorified backing singers. Even so, they carefully studied each other and critiqued their lip-synching. Used to belting out songs in chorus lines, neither of them could be accused of under-selling as they were used to having to get on top of full orchestras.

However, when scrutinising each other, it soon became obvious that a performance for cameras that would be close up necessitated a more restrained delivery. The lyrics had to be 'acted' a little more and they soon learned that their instinct to open their mouths as fully as if they were singing live was both unnecessary and somewhat unconvincing as their vocals were turned down quite significantly in the final mix. Claude arrived in the early afternoon in a panic of frustration.

'I have been sitting in front of a mirror all morning! I just look dumb when I try to mime – like some teenage girl singing into a hairbrush.' His brow was furrowed with annoyance. Satine and Ava patiently coaxed him to relax into the sort of dialled-back delivery that he had been giving. His full lips had seemed to chew up the lyrics as he mimed at first, but eventually, he took on board what they were trying to get across to him. Nevertheless, it was the evening before they felt anything comfortable with the prospect of being filmed the following day. All three were heartily sick of the song too by the time they broke for food.

Glen had called Ava in the early evening with promises of his return at the weekend. However, the two-minute call had only left Ava more frustrated and she sank into a brooding silence whilst Satine and Claude had their final run-throughs. Claude had choreographed a dance for himself – mainly to occupy the large swathes in the three-minute song where he was not singing at all. He gyrated and dipped to the disco beat with captivating finesse, pouting beautifully as he stomped back and forth.

'The girls are going to love you!' Satine clapped as Claude took a bow. 'The boys will love you too!' She added this much to Claude's delight. Claude frowned at this, saying:

'I will have to pretend that it is girls, girl, girls all the way for me.' Ava and Satine looked at each other, both knowing that Claude was right. There was no point trying to contradict or patronise him: pop music inhabited a world that was very simple and very heterosexual, at least in outward appearance. There were no openly gay singers in pop groups. Rosie had already put it on the line that even the girls in a group would have to be 'officially single.' Young fans all needed to buy into the dream that their pop idols could be their future husband or wife and for that, they had to seem to be straight and single. Keeping a boyfriend or girlfriend out of the limelight would be a challenge for a straight star and they ran the risk of losing favour with some fans who needed their crush to be theirs and theirs alone. But gay? That would kill the career stone dead. Satine gave Claude a hug and said:

'Don't worry about anything, baby boy. We will cross all the bridges we have to when we come to them.' Claude smiled thoughtfully. Then, without further word, he rewound the tape and went through his dance routine again. Nothing could get Claude down for long, Satine thought. However, she found that she was thinking and worrying about him long into the night.

Rosie ripped through the apartment like a tornado the following morning, reminding both women of their first meeting with her all those weeks ago. She has bustled them into Wieler's Mercedes, clucking like a deranged hen all the time. Wieler picked up both Claude and Cicely from outside the recording studio before heading out of town and into the countryside. The day was bright and sunny, showing off the densely forested terrain beautifully. After about half an hour, the car pulled off the main road and down a bumpy dirt track. The trees gave way to farmland and soon they came to a stop outside a huge barn. It had clearly been converted from its original use and had an array of beautiful bay windows and an imposing wooden door with etched glass panels. As soon as the car came to a stop, the door was flung open to reveal S.K. Behind him stood the same tiny make-up artist who had, if anything, grown shorter and uglier since they had last seen him. S.K. waved imperiously at them and then disappeared back inside the barn. Rumpelstiltskin stood and watched the occupants of the car disembark, shaking his gargoyle head disapprovingly.

The interior of the barn was taken up by a large stage in one corner and an array of recording and mixing equipment to rival that in S.K.'s studio. There was a small recreational area with sofas and a kitchenette. Two doors off the main area led to dressing rooms and Satine, Cicely, Ava and Claude were quickly ushered into them by Rumpelstiltskin. Their group costumes were hanging ready for them in addition to an array of wigs. The second she saw the wigs, Satine saw red: she had already told Rosie that she detested wearing them. She turned to look for Rosie, only to see that she was standing right behind her and had noticed Satine observe the wigs. Before Satine could open her mouth, Rosie launched into one of her simpering tones:

'I know. I know! But S.K. really thinks that a little more…movement with a lovely long wig would really work on camera. Why don't you at least give one of them a try and see? They are very good quality. Silk caps and real hair – the best that you can buy.'

As Satine looked at Rosie, and for all the woman's coaxing and apparently reasonable manner, all she could see was the face of the racist thug hiding in his fast car. Rosie imagined herself to be corporate charm personified, but what was the real difference in the message she was trying to put across and the intentions or the brain-dead youth? He had believed himself entitled to abuse her and Lukas based on some notion of racial superiority. Here, Satine was being made to feel that she was somehow being difficult if she objected to hiding away a fundamental part of herself. She thought of the very few black women that appeared on the television screens when she was growing up. Images of

Motown singers on Top of the Pops were the only ones she could conjure – all of them wearing long, straight wigs. Even when represented, women of colour like herself were somehow altered to be, what? More palatable? Less different? Now, here she stood, like all of them hoping that she would soon be on Top of the Pops too. And she was going to allow someone to dictate to her that looking somehow more 'white' was a good idea? She looked Rosie straight in the eye, pausing to dial down her instinct to shout. She imagined her mother and the way that she would quietly but firmly speak her truth.

'Rosie. If S.K. likes those wigs so very much, I suggest that he starts wearing one of them.'

'But,-' Rosie's words died in her throat as she took in the glint in Satine's eyes.

'I am a black woman. I have a black woman's hair. I happen to think it is beautiful.'

'Oh.' Fear helped Rosie locate her vocal chords. 'Oh, my dear! Of course you are beautiful. In every way. It was just that –'

'It was just that you and S.K. would prefer I conformed to a white woman's ideal of beauty rather than my own. And yet, you pretend that the racial diversity in Mixed Emotions is something you value.'

'B-but it is! It is!' Satine had never seen Rosie blush before and savoured every second of it. She continued to look steadily at Rosie, determined that the woman would have to fill the very tense air between them if it took all day. Rosie looked about herself, vainly hoping that she would attract the attention of S.K. Finally, she spoke:

'I am sorry. It will never happen again.'

The simplicity of Rosie's words were not what Satine had expected. Nor did she realise how much she needed to hear them until they were spoken. She regarded Rosie for a few moments longer, before nodding her head slowly and turning away. In her mind, she could see Iodine nodding in approval.

Cicely had been given a new beaded headpiece that reached her shoulders. Although it looked quite beautiful in the way it framed her high cheek bones, Cicely told Satine that the garment was very badly made and was digging into her scalp in several places. Claude was told he would be bare-chested throughout the film and Stiltskin set about applying black mascara to Claude's chest hair to ensure that it was picked up sufficiently on camera.

The filming itself was remarkably smooth. S.K. had employed two cameramen for the day and they took up different positions from each other during the filming. Their films would be edited together later, Rosie announced, so that the finished film was interesting and not static. Claude's dance routine went down very well with everyone, securing him close-ups during the instrumental break after the middle eight. It seemed that S.K. shared Satine's prediction that Claude's moves would be a secret weapon to harness female fans and he kept shouting 'gut' as Claude dipped and spun to the tape.

Cicely was filmed under a single spotlight for the opening refrain, and she performed it with considerable charisma. Her lip-synching was perfect from the start, and she had clearly understood the need to restrain the delivery and 'act' the lyrics to the camera. Satine and Ava wondered if she had spent the previous day figuring it out the hard way, but they suspected that she had probably nailed it straight away.

The filming concluded with the group members introducing themselves by name and adding a trilling 'and we are Mixed Emotions!' Rosie said that particular segment could be used on trailers to music shows if needed. Despite their seemingly endless wait to get into the recording studio and the horrors of the raid and its legacy, Satine and Ava both felt that this was finally the start of the dream.

Wieler had sat and watched the whole day's work with interest. As they got back into the Mercedes that evening, he turned around in the driver's seat and announced:

'I think that you will all have a Mercedes of your own this time next year.'

With that, his face lit up in the first uncontained smile that they had ever seen on his face. This, along with the fact that they were starting to feel like proper pop stars after the day's filming meant that Ava and Satine were as buoyant as they had felt in a very long time. The nightmare of the raid and the endless waiting seemed to be easier to dismiss that evening. Ava's mood was enhanced further by the huge bouquet of flowers that had been delivered during the day that rested against the door of the apartment building. The card was from Cooper, promising that he would make up for lost time with Ava very soon. Satine was catching up rapidly with her friend in the smitten stakes and another night with Lukas planned for that evening.

Over the next few days, the apartment was never without the sound of the radio. Weiler would knock on their door and announce if the song was being played on regional stations, whilst Ava and Satine kept a close ear to the national stations. S.K. had certainly done his work, as the song was played constantly and to enthusiastic reception by the D.J.s. It was even starting to be requested by members of the public who phoned in to the local stations – (they would find out later that many of those calls were made by Rosie and S.K. themselves). The new top 40 listing for the end of that week saw the single debut at number 33. To the group members, this seemed only partially impressive, but Rosie assured all concerned that this was a superb placing and even S.K. had anticipated that the song would initially debut outside of the top 40. This was, Rosie announced, the most crucial time for the single and she warned them all not to expect to get any sleep in the next working week as publicity was more crucial than ever to keep the momentum building.

That Saturday night brought with it the promised return of Glen Cooper. He arrived at the apartment carrying another bouquet and a bottle of champagne. He had booked a swanky restaurant for himself and Ava, but insisted that Satine and Lukas shared the champagne with them before he whisked her away.

'To Mixed Emotions!' Cooper raised his glass and wrapped his free arm around Ava's shoulders, hugging her close and planting a kiss on the top of her head. 'To superstardom!'

'To superstardom!' Lukas echoed, directing his dimpled smile at Satine and blowing her a kiss. Ava seemed lost in the delight of the moment, gazing at Cooper with Bambi eyes. Satine flinched slightly at this, as she was beginning to grow impatient with the way that Cooper kept her friend hanging around. She had tried to broach the subject, but Ava always defended Cooper and the demands of his job that kept him away. This irritated Satine even more than Cooper's actual absences: Ava had never been one to sit around waiting for the telephone to ring, but now she seemed to be so much in this man's thrall that her happiness seemed to be defined by him rather too much. Even the showy champagne toasting rankled with Satine a little that evening. She had thought that her feelings had been carefully hidden, but after the couple had departed for their date, Lukas made it clear that he had picked up on Satine's mood:

'What don't you like about Glen?' The question was so direct that Satine flushed for a moment at the words. She looked at Lukas a little awkwardly at first, but was mollified by the expression on his face that indicated there was no judgement or criticism in his question.

'Mm,' Satine began, 'I'm really not sure. He seems perfectly charming -when he's around.'

'You think he keeps Ava dangling?'

'Maybe. But it's more how crestfallen she is when he isn't around. It isn't really like her, you know?'

'Do you doubt his reasons about work?'

'No...I don't think so.' Satine found that she was finding her thoughts as she spoke and felt reassured by how easy it was to talk to Lukas. Most pleasingly, he was allowing her time to think. After a few moments, when it was clear that Satine was not going to elaborate on her previous statement, Lukas ventured:

'Perhaps you haven't seen her this in love before?' Satine smiled at Lukas's words. He had a knack of cutting to the heart of the matter that was very refreshing.

'It could be that, yes. Ava was always the one that men went crazy for back home. She never seemed to be so bothered with them. She enjoyed the power, I guess.'

'Cupid gets us all in the end.' Lukas leaned over and planted a kiss on Satine's lips. 'Thank God,' he added.

Cooper looked at his reflection in the mirror of the restaurant bathroom and gave himself a reassuring wink. The awkwardness he expected after his absence had not materialised and the champagne and flowers had done their work on Ava. She had sat dewy eyes through the first two courses, and he kept reaching out and touching her hand as she told him about the latest new about Mixed Emotions. It seemed like the group was starting to make its mark, which made things even more urgent. His ears were still ringing from Dakin's latest tirade that afternoon: as far as the old goat was concerned, this was Cooper's last chance to come up with the goods on Cicely. Once Mixed Emotions took off, they would be travelling non-stop. This would be a perfect way for Cooper to pull the plug on the relationship and play the 'abandoned boyfriend' card and the thought pleased him no end. However, it also meant that Ava's usefulness as a link to Cicely was also about to come to an end. Dakin knew this too and had knitted together an impressive string of expletives that left Cooper in no doubt that he had no more than a fortnight before he was on a plane back to Australia. A good result would secure promotion, but without it Cooper knew that he would suffer the consequences long after Dakin had retired. There was no time left to be particularly subtle, which is why Cooper returned to their table and asked Ava the following:

'When you get huge, do you think everyone will cope with the attention?'

Ava was a little taken aback by the abruptness of his question and thought for a while before answering.

'I think Claude will breeze through, as long as the press don't take too much of an interest in his private life. Satine has Lukas now and I think she will be cool.'

'And you have me!' Cooper did the hand holding again as he said this and Ava returned the expected smile. 'And what about Cicely?'

'Mm,' Ava was lost in thought for a moment. 'Cicely is much harder to read. I like her, much more than I did at first. But there's an…aloofness to her sometimes. A disconnect from the rest of us, I guess you could say. We bonded more after we had that meal together and, well, as vile as the raid on the club was, it did bringing us closer. But there is still..' Ava looked around, as if the right words would appear in the air. 'There is still a…distance, I guess you'd call it.'

'Does that worry you?'

'Sometimes…but she's very professional and calm. Why?'

'Oh, I don't know,' Cooper pretended to be pondering too and hesitated before he said the words that he had formed whilst in the bathroom: 'It's just that there is going to be so much pressure on you all from the press. You and Satine know each other inside out, but Cicely…well, I just wouldn't like there to be anything in the background that could spoil things.'

'Strange thing to say! Like what?' Her eyes looked sharp and Cooper realised that he had overplayed his hand a little.

'Oh, probably nothing. I just wouldn't want anything to get in the way of you all enjoying becoming superstars!' He leaned forward and gave Ava his best smouldering look: 'I think I am just a little insecure about my gorgeous girl leaving me behind.'

'Well,' Ava laughed, 'order us another bottle of that fabulous wine and I will think about keeping you on when I am ruling the universe!'

Cooper sensibly avoided mentioning Cicely for the rest of the evening and was careful not to turn down Ava's invitation to stay the night. Their love-making was an enjoyable perk of the job and long overdue, Cooper decided. And besides, it stopped him thinking about Dakin for a few hours. However, as he came for the second time that night, it suddenly occurred to him that he should have bedded Ava weeks before. It wasn't that the sex had been particularly great, but it seemed now that it might have been a good idea to have spent more time at her apartment in order to have placed a bug. Then again, such things were expensive and notoriously unreliable in the first place. Cooper had to supress a little shudder as the image of Dakin's face loomed into his post-orgasmic haze. There would not be a third orgasm that night.

The days leading up to the next chart listings being announced were a whirl of radio interviews and performances. The recorded film of the performance was shown on national television several times and on three different channels. In the radio stations, Cicely was encouraged by Rosie to do the majority of the talking. Inevitably, they were asked if there was 'anyone special' in their lives and the party line was that all the women were single and 'currently too busy with Mixed Emotions' to have time for romance. Claude was almost convincing in his scripted response of 'I have not met the right girl yet' and 'work has to come first before love. Besides, I have three beautiful women at my side the whole time!' The latter was an especially cringe-worthy line that Rosie had been inordinately proud of thinking up. Claude could only imagine how trite the lines Rosie had rejected must have been. However, trite or not, the radio stations seemed to love it all. By the time it came for the new chart run down, all of the group members had lost count of the times they had been told that the song would definitely have risen into the top ten – if not the top five!

So it was with universal optimism that Mixed Emotions, Lukas, Weiler and Rosie sat around the recording studio conference room as they listened to the chart rundown. S.K. was 'scouting venues' and 'working on the next single' according to Rosie. The song was not in the first section of the countdown from 40 to 30, which was a very good sign. When it did not appear in the second section from 29 to 20, the mood in the room was buoyant. Mixed Emotions still did not appear in the first half of the top twenty. Ten to six came and went. The room grew silent as they listened to the DJ make the announcement that none of them had dared to dream could be possible:

'Ahead of the top five, we can tell you that there is a brand new number one today!'

Rosie translated this to Ava and Satine and they clutched each other tightly. It would be pretty unheard of for a new band to leap from number 37 right up to the top five in one single week, but there it was, unfolding as they listened. Song number five came and went, as did number four.

'Oh my God, we're in the top three!' Claude whooped.

Number three was played next, but it was not Mixed Emotions. The number one from last week was now down to number two. Agonisingly, the DJ then did a complete countdown of the songs from 40 to 2. Then came the announcement:

'And moving up from last week's number three, this is our brand new number one.......'

Rosie switched off the radio before the song even began. All of them sat in mute and shocked stillness for what seemed an eternity. In the minutes before the countdown had taken them to the announcement of the new number one, all of them had seen their future as a glittering success. The reality of what they had actually heard did not and would not sink in until Rosie made a call to the radio station to be informed that Mixed Emotions had sold well midweek but had then petered off and was currently number 43 in the new chart listing. Cicely had gone outside to get some air at hearing the news, betraying very little emotion as she slipped from the room. Rosie inhaled half of a freshly lit cigarette in one go, angrily crushing the remainder into the ashtray that was already over-flowing in front of her on the conference table. Satine and Ava sobbed quietly, Lukas trying and failing to mutter comforting words.

Chapter Ten – And we are all but playthings of the Gods

The weekend did not alleviate the sense of numbness that Satine had been struck with when the reality of the song's failure had finally started to sink in, despite Lukas's attempt to move her towards a more philosophical viewpoint. He had pointed out over and over that reaching the top 40 at all for a new group was quite an achievement. Furthermore, the German charts were only one of many and, as far as the industry was concerned, the UK and America were far more important. S.K. had been quite sanguine about the whole affair, Rosie was keen to tell them in the wake of their disappointment. This all seemed too little in the face of what had happened for Satine, and she put off the weekly call home to Iodine for as long as she could. Even when she did muster up the strength to talk to her mother, she avoided the topic of the single completely, electing to say that everything was 'moving in the right direction.' If Iodine detected the truth of Satine's feelings, she did not let on but Satine would not have been surprised if her voice had betrayed the reality of how events had left her feeling.

Ava had seemed more upbeat that Satine over the weekend. Glen had been suitably sympathetic when she had told him about the chart fiasco and promised to take her out for a sumptuous lunch that Monday which kept her spirits up. However, Satine had to manage without Lukas who had been enlisted to drive S.K. to several meetings throughout the weekend. According to Rosie, all was far from lost but the single needed a wider release outside of Germany and fast. New songs needed to be trawled through too in order to capitalise on the buzz (however brief) that had been generated by the top 40 placing. Rosie had driven them mad with her own mantra of 'a hit is a hit is a HIT' and they were relieved that the weekend had required nothing more than an early photo call for an interview that had already been done. Even Weiler had attempted some homespun philosophy when he had told them that 'the wheel may have wobbled, but has not yet fallen off the bus.' This was backed up by and endless extended metaphor about the 'journey' of the group and the 'fuel' of commitment and resolve. After twenty minutes, both Ava and Satine had prayed that the former, taciturn Weiler would make a comeback.

The first caller at their apartment on Monday was not Glen Cooper. At around ten o'clock, whilst both women were still in their robes and lounging around there came an urgent hammering on the front door from the street below. They heard Weiler opening the door and speaking in German with someone. Moments later, Lotte appeared at their apartment door. She was dressed in jeans and a thick jumper and carried a huge rucksack. Both Ava and Satine were immediately aware of what Lotte's appearance meant:

'You're leaving? Today?' Ava hugged Lotte and the two of them stood in a silent embrace for a few moments. Satine followed suit and then the two of them ushered Lotte in to sit down. Lotte lit a cigarette and began to talk to them both. She was very serious in both her expression and tone, which alarmed both Satine and Ava:

'I am flying back home this afternoon. Rosie tried to talk me into staying on, but she can go straight to hell! S.K. can shove it all up his fat arsehole too!'

It was clear that she was fighting to remain as composed as possible. They were used to Lotte being volatile at the mention of Rosie, but her ill-supressed unease was clearly something much more serious that morning. They were not surprised at the fact that Lotte was returning home as she had threatened as much after the raid. Had they not been caught up in the now seemingly broken dream of Mixed

Emotions, Ava and Satine would probably have come to a similar conclusion. Nor did Lotte have the pull of romance to keep her in Hanover.

'I'm really sorry to see you go, Lotte,' Ava began, 'but I'm not surprised. You heard about what happened with the single? We might not be far behind you if things don't work out.'

'I heard. Sorry.' Lotte smiled weakly at them both before turning her gaze upon Ava. When she spoke next there was a nervous catch to her voice that neither Ava or Satine had ever heard before from their typically confident friend:

'I have something to tell you before I leave, Ava.' She looked down at the ground for a moment before continuing. 'It will not be easy to hear.'

'Should I leave you alone?' Satine asked, but was relieved when Lotte shook her head in response.

'Christ, Lotte! You're scaring me!' Ava snapped.

'Sorry,' Lotte held her hands up in a placatory gesture. 'I don't mean to be melodramatic here. I just want you to be prepared. Okay. The thing is that I got a letter from Tam yesterday. She is out on bail, but it is not looking good as far as getting the stupid charges dropped.'

'I'm so sorry,' Ava began but then noticed Lotte's expression darken and she fell silent again. Lotte looked directly at Ava and continued, her pace quickening as she spoke as if she were going to lose the will to articulate her news at any moment:

'The night of the raid, Tamara got separated from us, remember? She was sick and they took her to get cleaned up. While she was on the corridor on her way back to the cells, she saw,' she looked away for a second and then turned her gaze back to Ava. 'She saw your boyfriend.'

'Glen? But that's not right. He was out of town when the raid happened and –' Ava's words were silenced by Lotte holding up her hand.

'He was there, Ava. And he looked very much to Tam like he was there on business. She recognised him and she is certain he recognised her but chose not to. The next thing she knows, Tam is shipped out and deported. Out of all the girls arrested that night, it was Tam that got singled out. You have to ask yourself why that would happen. And drugs! There might be any number of dancers at that rathole club who take, deal or supply on the quiet -who knows? But Tam is the last person who would get mixed up in anything.'

'Could Tam have been mistaken? It was such a crazy night and we were all terrified and strung out.' Lotte was a little surprised that these words came from Satine rather than Ava. Lotte kept her eye on Ava, noticing that the look of shock was mixed with something else – the dawning of a reluctant acceptance, but an acceptance, nevertheless. Lotte continued:

'I'm sorry, Ava. But it's the truth. Glen Cooper is mixed up in this somehow. I don't want to hurt your feelings, but there it is. Tam's life is on the line here if she gets convicted. She will lose her children, and I don't think she would survive that – even if she could survive prison, which I doubt.' Lotte sat back and waited for Ava to respond. Once again, it was Satine who spoke first:

'I just don't get any of this! How could Glen be involved in what happened to Tam? It just doesn't make sense.'

'I'm very much afraid it might make a lot of sense.'

Both Lotte and Satine were stunned to hear Ava articulate the words -partly because the content was so unexpected and because her tone was so flat and somehow definite.

'Ava?' Satine reached her hand out to touch Ava's arm, but she shrugged it away and took it to her feet. Pacing back and forth, her arms wrapped tightly around her torso, Ava began to mumble to herself in a manner that seemed to indicate she had become suddenly oblivious to the fact that Lotte and Satine were still in the room. Then, after a few moments of stillness, Ava darted into the bathroom. Satine and Lotte could hear the sound of the shower being turned on and could only look at each other helplessly.

'Tam hasn't got it wrong, Satine.' Lotte frowned. Satine nodded slowly as she replied:

'No, I don't think she has. And I think Ava knows that too.' Satine looked anxiously at the bathroom door. 'The thing is – what is she going to do? Glen is due here in a couple of hours to take her out to lunch.'

'Shit.' Lotte's reply was, as usual, pithy and remarkably apt in the circumstances. 'I can't hang around – but that's probably just as well. I could kill the bastard!'

'You'll have to get in line,' Satine frowned.

A few minutes later, when Ava burst out of the bathroom in a cloud of steam and bolted into her bedroom, slamming the door behind her with thundering force. The sound of her hairdryer and the clattering of coat hangers followed.

'I didn't want to have to be the one to burst her bubble here, you know?' Lotte said as she lit another cigarette. 'But I couldn't leave knowing what I know. Whoever that bastard really is and whatever he's up to, I couldn't leave Ava at his mercy after what happened to Tam – what could *still* happen to Tam!'

'I know that Lotte. I'm going to miss you. Ava will miss you too.' Satine battled to give Lotte her attention as she spoke, but she could not help gazing at Ava's bedroom door.

'What do you think she will do?'

'My guess is that she will confront him. How can I stop her?'

'You can't,' Lotte frowned. 'But I doubt she'll get the truth out of the bastard. I just hope he doesn't talk her round. She's very smitten, I think. And he's certainly got charm.'

'This is all such a mess!' Satine stalked into the kitchen area with this and poured two very large glasses of wine for herself and Lotte. She gave the clock on the wall a guilty glance but quickly decided that the sun was over the yardarm somewhere in the world. Lotte took the glass from Satine when she held it out to her without a word and gulped down about a third of its contents. Satine slumped back down on the sofa and did a similar thing – although in her case she had probably managed to drain half of the glass in one. The two women sat in silence for a while, each engaged in their mission to reach the bottom of their glasses. Suddenly, Ava's bedroom door flew open and she burst back into the lounge. Her hair, hastily dried, was tousled and she had applied a thick layer of make-up and a very dark red lipstick. She wore jeans and a baggy black top. Satine had to smile to herself that, even in a maelstrom of shock and potential heartbreak, Ava looked beautiful.

'So – will I pass muster?' Ava demanded.

'Absolutely!' Satine jumped up and held her depleted wine glass out towards Ava. Ava shook her head at the offer. 'Are you sure you still want to see him? I mean, don't you want more time to think about what you are going to say?'

'More time is the last thing I need. I have to know the truth today.'

'He might not tell you.' Lotte's bluntness was apt, but Satine was glad that she had not been the one to have said it to Ava.

'No..' Ava nodded her head slightly, lost in thought for a moment.

' No, you're absolutely right. But I have to try.'

Lotte announced that she would have to leave for the airport at that point, hugging them both and vowing that she would come back to visit them – wherever they might be in the future. She wrote her parent's address on the notepad that they had on the kitchen counter and, stifling a tear, she breezed out of the apartment. After she had gone, Satine and Ava sat anxiously until the clock ticked round to twelve o'clock – the time when Glen Cooper was due to call for Ava.

At three minutes past twelve, Cooper knocked on their door.

'Are you sure you want to do this?' Satine shot an anxious glance at Ava.

'Yes,' Ava was on her feet and moving towards the door as she spoke. 'Go into your bedroom for a second. I won't bring him in here.'

Satine nodded and gave Ava a quick hug of support before ducking into her room. Seconds later she heard the door open and Cooper's voice. A short time after, the door was closed again from the outside. Satine sat on the corner of her bed, knowing that she would not be able to function until Ava was walking back through the door.

……

Ava noticed that Glen had booked the same restaurant that he had taken her to on their first date all those months ago. She was sure that she would have considered that to be a wonderfully thoughtful and romantic gesture if only it had happened a day earlier. Now it seemed like a lazy and cynical action. She had struggled to make light conversation in the taxi to the restaurant, but she was sure that Cooper had thought her quiet demeanour was attributable to the sudden turn of fortunes for Mixed Emotions. He had raised an eyebrow when she turned down a glass of white wine, but she mustered all of the acting skills she could to keep from screaming in his face. She drained her second glass of iced water, the numbness it gave to her mouth a fitting sensation to what she felt as she looked at Cooper. She could feel her inward, intense anger rise with every passing second. But who was she most angry with? Him? Or herself for still finding she could not stop thinking how remarkably beautiful he was? She tried to focus on a feature of his handsome face that she could decide she never liked, but it just wasn't possible. He was the fairy-tale prince, the stuff of dreams and the cover of 'Jackie' magazine from when she was a teenager. Ava dug her nails into the palm of her hand as she forced herself to face the truth about fairy-tales and magazine covers: they were all bullshit.

'It isn't over, you know.'

'What?' Ava was startled by Cooper's words. Did he know what was coming?

'Mixed Emotions. The Beatles didn't start off at number one.'

'Oh, yeah.' In that moment, Ava knew that she could not keep it in any longer. When she spoke, it felt like her voice was coming from inside and somewhere else in the room at the same time; she could almost watch herself from above as she said the words:

'You're not working on trains signalling at all, are you? You're police. Why did you lie to me? And what did you do to Tamara?'

The silence after she had spoken seemed to stretch out forever. She looked at the beautiful man before her without blinking. His face ran a range of expressions, from a stifled and seemingly incredulous little laugh to a furrowed brow of confusion. But, as she stared, she saw his eyes harden. His gaze dropped after a few moments when he realised she was not going to look away or speak again until he answered. And, most conclusively for Ava, she could see a tiny droplet of sweat snake its way down his forehead. Finally, Cooper spoke:

'Oh, Christ. Yes,' he began to look around the room as if trying to locate an exit from her gaze. 'Yes, I haven't told you the truth about everything. I work for Interpol.' At the sound of that last word, Ava removed any niggling doubt she might have wanted to cling onto somewhere in her mind. Although by no means clear on what exactly Interpol was or did outside of mention of it on cop shows, she knew that they were worldwide and powerful – certainly powerful enough to get someone deported at the drop of a hat. A waiter arrived at the table at that point, to be hastily dismissed by Cooper with a barked order to give them ten more minutes. Ava did not break her stare as he did so, and Cooper leaned forward and began to speak in a whisper:

'It is a very serious case. I could not tell you the truth about what I do – but I wasn't lying about how I feel about you!' With this, he attempted to reach out for Ava, but she pulled back on her chair and out of his reach. The legs of the chair made a shrill squeaking noise as she did this, and the restaurant fell suddenly silent at the unexpected sound. Moments later, the typical lunch hubbub resumed and the disturbance was forgotten.

'Just tell me why.' Ava battled to keep her voice even as she spoke. 'Why did you have to lie to me?'

'Because…because I needed to get close to someone in your circle. Without you becoming suspicious. I would have told you everything when I could. I have my orders too – I couldn't just do what I wanted.' He looked imploringly at Ava. Had he not attempted a supercilious grin at that point, Ava may have found herself weakening. However, this gesture only served to anger her more. When she spoke, her tone was glacial:

'It's Cicely. Isn't it?'

Cooper looked down at his hands and then back up at Ava. This was confirmation enough.

'You used me to get to her, didn't you? Of course you did. It makes sense now why you were so interested in how we got along. You wanted me to get information from her or about her. Claude is just a farm boy, really. What could he have ever done? Satine and I are an open book. No, it's Cicely you're after.'

'She's not what you think she is, baby.'

'Don't call me that. Don't ever call me that again.' Ava stood up began to turn away, but Cooper sprang to his feet and caught her arm, turning her round to face him.

'Ava! Please! I had no choice but to lie about what I did. But I haven't lied about how I feel about you!'

'I told you – I don't want to hear it! Stay away from me from now on and, if you have any decency at all, do something to help Tamara!'

'I will, okay! I will but just sit down and talk to me!' Cooper's desperation only angered Ava more and she pushed him away and marched towards the exit. No longer conscious of the rest of the diners, Cooper shouted after Ava:

'At least ask her what she did, Ava! Ask her and then you'll know why I had to do all of this. Ask Cicely!'

Cooper's last words to Ava rang in her ears throughout the journey back to the apartment. The rain was lashing down as she exited the taxi that had brought her back to an anxious Satine. The two of them sat close to each other as Ava related the events in the restaurant. She accepted a large glass of wine from Satine as she repeated Cooper's pathetic attempts to calm her down after she had made her accusation.

'Interpol. That's serious, isn't it? I mean, what could they want Cicely for?' Satine remembered as she spoke the first time they had seen Cicely: before they even knew who she was, the beautiful vision that had boarded the plane late as they waited to make their flight to Hanover was still easy to recall. Her aloofness had just started to seem part of who she was, although she could be warm and funny too. Satine's mind was racing. Who was the real Cicely? What could she have done to cause Cooper to go to such destructive lengths and who was pulling his strings in the first place?

'There's only one thing we can do now.'

'Talk to Cicely?'

'Yes,' Ava said as she was making her way to the telephone. 'Talk to her right now!'

Cicely picked up after three rings and Ava was very circumspect in her speech, merely saying that there was an urgent crisis and they had to speak face to face with Cicely before the day was out. Cicely's reply was just 'I'll be there in half an hour' and she put the receiver down. Ava turned to Satine, the telephone still in her hand:

'That was easy.'

'She's coming over?' Satine asked.

'Straight away. Did I sound that menacing?'

'You sounded deadly serious, certainly. But maybe –'

'-Maybe she's been expecting this to happen at some point all along?' Ava finished Satine's sentence for her, echoing her friend's thoughts precisely. The next half an hour crawled by and they both had to battle with themselves to refrain from opening the third and only remaining bottle of wine in the refrigerator. 'Best wait till she gets here before we open that' Satine had said as she opened and closed the refrigerator door for the third time. Ava, nervously pacing up and down, nodded in agreement.

When Cicely arrived she looked as glamorous as ever, although it was evident to Satine and Ava that she had been a little more hasty in her application of make-up and lipstick than they were used to seeing. Equally, errant strands of her wiry fringe poked out from the edge of her silk turban and betrayed the fact that she has put it on in haste and without the assistance of a mirror. Her taxi had dropped her off at the corner of the block and Cicely had clearly forgotten to bring either an umbrella or a raincoat. The rain was lashing down and, although she had only had to run about twenty feet, her shoes and the cuffs of her slacks were sodden and the cotton kaftan top she wore was dark with rain spots. Ushering her to sit down, Cicely accepted a glass of wine from the eagerly anticipated bottle that Ava had opened the moment they heard Weiler open the door downstairs.

'You said that this was urgent.'

Cicely's voice was as calm and measured as ever, but her eyes were wide and both Satine and Ava knew that there was no need to delay getting to the point.

'I have just found out that Glen is working for Interpol.' Ava spoke quietly and let the words resonate.

Cicely took a sip of wine and looked downwards for a few moments. She looked levelly at Ava, as if she was going to make a reply but did say anything. Ava continued:

'He was using me to get to you, somehow. He said that you were not what you seemed. What did he mean?'

Cicely gave a little smile at the directness of Ava's words. He first question was initially surprising to Ava:

'Are you still seeing him?'

'God, no! We're over!'

'I'm sorry.' Cicely took another sip of her wine and looked away into the middle distance, as if she was taking herself out of the room and to somewhere far away.

'I need a bit more that 'sorry', Cicely! I want – I deserve some explanation!' Ava was angered by the apparent poise that Cicely was managing to maintain and felt patronised by her sympathy. At the tone of her voice, Cicely seemed to jerk back into the room and when she spoke her voice was quiet:

'You do. You deserve an explanation. I just need to know that I can trust you both with what I am about to tell you.'

'Trust! That's fucking rich, isn't it!?' Ava's anger was apt, but Satine quickly stepped in to calm her as she knew there was nothing to gain from antagonising Cicely:

'Okay, Ava! I know that this is a terrible situation, but let's not forget that Glen caused it. We need to listen to Cicely. We need to know the truth.'

Cicely nodded her silent thanks at Satine but maintained her focus on Ava as she continued:

'I will tell you the truth. But first, I need to know how much time Cooper spent here.'

'Why?' Ava looked at Cicely with genuine puzzlement at the question. Was she twisting the knife and trying to find out how involved she and Glen had been?

'You think he's bugged the place, don't you?' Satine said, reading Cicely's purpose. Cicely nodded eagerly at Satine and Ava realised what they both meant with a sigh.

'Oh, right. Well, no, he didn't spend any time here really, and certainly not any time alone.' Ava looked down as she added, 'and only one night.'

'Okay. I really am sorry I had to ask you that.' Cicely took another sip of wine and her eyes seemed to wander back to that distant place again. It was now clear that she was taking herself to the past. When she spoke, her voice had a wistful tone, and she seemed to be someone entirely different to the Cicely that Ava and Satine had encountered:

'It was years ago, back in '67. I was in Paris. I'd got a two month gig to sing at a club. Jazz stuff mostly. The club was seedy but it paid well enough. I'm fluent in French and I had some friends in Paris and so crashing on sofas was okay. It meant I didn't have to spent my earnings on rent, you know? Anyway, for the first couple of weeks it was okay. A few of the musicians tried it on, but most of the customers were with their wives or mistresses so I felt quite comfortable doing the shows.' She paused for a moment to sip her wine. Unbidden, Satine filled the glass up, to which Cicely nodded her thanks. Satine noted that Cicely was overusing 'okay' in a manner that betrayed how nervous she was as she related her tale. Taking a deep breath, Cicely continued:

'Anyway, towards the end of the second week the owner of the club started to show up. Phillipe Le Grande. Known as a local crook, but small-time. Or so I thought. He took a shine to me and seemed okay…until people at the club started taking me to one side and warning me off. He was very bad news, they said. I found out, much later, that he was a very big drug dealer.' She looked from Ava to Satine

263

at that point, her voice growing even quieter when she spoke again:

'I tried to keep it friendly and light, but he was getting more persistent. I thought it would be okay, I was nearing the end of the booking and I had a gig in Amsterdam lined up so there was no way I could be talked into staying on, even though he tried to talk me into it! One of the bar staff used to give me a ride back to my friends at the end of the night and the bar manager used to let us both duck out a little early to avoid Le Grande where possible. It didn't always work, but they had my back as much as they dared. He was not a good man, and everyone was rightfully scared of pissing him off.' She took a sizeable gulp of her wine before she continued. Satine noticed that the knuckles on Cicely's hand started to protrude as she tightened her grip around the stem of the glass.

'Anyway. It was three nights before I was due to play my last set at the club. The girl who took me home called in sick and so I had to wait around for a taxi. Worse still, Le Grande was in, and he had been drinking heavily. He was a nasty man and an even nastier drunk. One of the waitresses had spilt his drink as she put in on the table and he fired her on the spot that night. He asked me to go to a bar with him that he owned, just for a drink, he said. He wanted to thank me for the work I had done. I refused as politely as I could and left. I was trying to flag down a taxi on the street, but nothing stopped for ages. Eventually, one did but when I went to get it, Le Grande was sitting in the back seat. He'd come looking for me. He said there was a little farewell party planned for me.'

'You went?' Ava's tone was sneering.

'I know how it sounds, Ava. But I was scared not to go. The taxi driver had obviously been paid a hefty chunk of cash and wasn't going to interfere. I tried to convince myself that a crowded bar would be okay, that I could slip away. We got to this bar and he said he was going to take us straight up to the executive lounge where there was champagne waiting. I said no, but he told me his wife was already up there with some of her friends. I should have run, but I didn't. So, I followed up to this supposed 'executive lounge.' It was a grotty little flat. An empty flat. I tried to get away the moment I saw it, but he grabbed me. There was a bed. He pushed me towards it but I got away from him at first. He blocked the door and threw me into the wall as I tried to push him out of the way. He was so strong! He was not going to stop until he got what he wanted.' Cicely looked from Ava to Satine. 'But I had a knife. He didn't count on that.'

'You…killed him?' Ava asked. Cicely nodded and stood up as she continued, walking to the lounge window and gazing at the rush hour traffic below her as the rain continued to lash down.

'He was either unconscious or dead when I left him. I think he was dead. I don't remember how it happened, but the knife was buried deep in his chest.'

'And you didn't go to the police?' Satine asked, but with no tone of criticism or accusation. Cicely shook her head.

'No. No police. Le Grande was too dangerous. Too well-connected for the police to protect me, I knew that, even if they did believe me about what the bastard tried to do!' She exhaled sharply. 'So, I set the place alight. Two days later I was in Amsterdam.'

'Just like that?' Ava asked, her voice catching angrily.

'No, Ava, not just like that!' Cicely came to sit down again as she spoke, looking deep into Ava's eyes as she finished her tale:

'I was terrified! I still am! I've been questioned over and over again – the last time was at Heathrow on the day we all flew here. They have no evidence, and I will not confess to ridding the world of that monster! I knew he was bad at the time, but I've found out so much more since then about the misery he caused; the lives he ruined with his drug empire must be in the thousands.'

Ava looked away for a few moments, and when she turned to look at Cicely again her eyes were glistening.

'No,' Ava said, nodding her head slowly. 'No. You did nothing wrong.'

Cicely closed her eyes in exhausted relief at the sound of Ava's words. Ava now walked to the window, massaging her temples as she battled to process what she had heard.

'We will never speak of this again – to anyone. The past stays in the past from now on,' Ava announced after a prolonged silence, turning to look at Cicely and Satine in turn as she spoke. Both women nodded their accord, and the silence descended again for a time. They knew that 'the past' meant Glen Cooper as well. 'And now,' she added, 'I need some air and more wine. Lots more wine.'

'It's still raining,' Satine advised.

'Then I'll take an umbrella.'

Frau Elsa Gurtzmore-Krause had not been having a good Monday. Two of the accounts that she thought were in the bag for her florist shop (weekly fresh flowers for a local hotel reception area and a similar arrangement for an uptown restaurant) had been abruptly pulled when a rival shop had undercut her offer. She was sure that she could get the account back for the hotel with a little negotiation, but the restaurant was adamant that they were happy with the rival offer. Elsa Gurtzmore-Krause knew her stock was the best around, and that her regular customers also knew that very well. Still, it hurt to see the way business was going these days; nobody could be assumed to be as good as their word.

Despite her low mood, Elsa Gurtzmore-Krause was cheered by the prospect of a cosy night in with her husband and the beautiful dinner he would be preparing for her even now, as she drove along the usual route home from the city centre location of her shop. The traffic had been its usual busy self that Monday, compounded by the heavy rain. However, Elsa Gurtzmore-Krause was an excellent and very steady driver. She always gave other vehicles plenty of room and was scrupulous in her observation of the speed limit. So it was that, when Ava stepped out from the kerbside and directly into her path, Elsa Gurtzmore-Krause was able to tell the traffic police, (albeit through her sobs) that she knew with a clear conscience that there was absolutely nothing she could have done to avoid hitting the poor young woman. Elsa Gurtzmore-Krause could only wish that the woman had walked the two hundred yards to the designated crossing rather than cross the street at such a dangerous spot. But then, Elsa Gurtzmore-Krause concluded correctly, it was raining heavily and the poor girl probably just wanted to get to and from the shops as quickly as possible. We all did it from time to time, and we usually got away with it. The traffic police agreed with her completely, saying that people often forgot that being struck head on by a vehicle that was travelling at a mere twenty-five kilometres an hour could still cause an instantly fatal head injury, as indeed it had on this sad occasion. Elsa Gurtzmore-Krause had asked if she could send flowers to the young woman's relatives, but the nice officer said that he thought the woman was a British national with no family in Hanover.

....

Two weeks later, Satine turned away from the graveside to look over her shoulder. Lukas held her hand tightly, turning with her to follow the direction of her gaze. The crowd behind Ava was only fitting and she recognised many faces from the chorus line of 'Nero!' in addition to scores of Ava's family and friends. Unexpectedly, Mrs Shorvosky stood just behind her in a black, veiled hat. Mrs Shorvosky gave her a small nod and a tight, sympathetic smile. The news of the accident had made the evening news and bulletins had even carried a clip of the 'Mixed Emotions' video. This had alerted people who would not have necessarily been contacted by the family and secured such a huge turnout at the service. Ava's family were, obviously, beyond devastated but both they and Satine were bowled over by the fact that Mr Dead had moved heaven and earth to get the red tape sorted and Ava returned to England for burial. He had also insisted on picking up what would have been a not inconsiderable bill to make the necessary arrangements.

Claude and Weiler had travelled to England to represent Mixed Emotions (Rosie's offer was rejected rather bluntly by Satine and Weiler had diplomatically stepped into the frame). As the crowds began to disperse towards their various vehicles, Satine found herself dropping back and letting go of Lukas's hand. He frowned, but she told her that he should walk back to the car with Claude. She gave Claude a little smile, noticing that he stood with Tamara and her children. The charges against Tamara had been suddenly dropped in the wake of Ava's death. Satine would never know if this was also something to do with Mr Dead and his family's influence, or perhaps Cooper finally showing a conscience and an attempt the assuage guilt. Satine would always hate Cooper for the fact that Ava had been taken whilst still in a mire of grief over the way he had used her to get to Cicely. She doubted that she would ever set eyes on him again, and for his sake she hoped that would be the case. Satine stood still for a time, closing her eyes and feeling the cool breeze on her face.

'She will always be a beautiful young angel now. Time will not ravage her. No consolation now, but in time maybe…'

Satine opened her eyes and turned to the sound of the voice. Weiler stood beside her, his eyes hidden by dark sunglasses but the tracks of tears visible beneath them on his cheeks. Satine smiled weakly. She had come to like him quite considerably, she realised. He had certainly been fond of Ava in his strange yet genuine way.

'So?'

Weiler's single word question was sufficient. Satine realised in that moment that it was entirely fitting that Weiler would be the one to ask it – not Claude or even Lukas. They would not ever have asked, for fear that the question itself would sway her decision to something that she would later regret and, potentially, blame them about. But Weiler? For all his brusque and seemingly hard edges, there was something sage in both his manner and the way in which he had chosen the time to confront Satine. Weiler removed his sunglasses, blinking his red raw eyes into focus and looked directly at Satine. She returned his gaze before smiling sadly and saying:

'Tell Rosie and S.K. I am staying here.'

Weiler made no reply. Instead, he leaned forward and kissed her softly on the forehead and then turned and walked away.

Epilogue

England – One Year Later

Satine vowed that she was not going to allow Iodine to pile her plate quite so high next time as she felt like she had gained six pounds since her arrival at her mother's house that afternoon. But there was no denying the beauty of Iodine's cooking and the feeling that every bite was made with love and sheer joy that Satine was back home in England. She could hear her mother rattling pots and pans as the washing-up was underway. As always, she had refused to allow Satine to help. Satine needed all her strength for two evening performances and a matinee, Iodine reminded her, as she wrestled the tea towel from her daughter's hands. Besides, Top of the Pops had already started as she knew that Satine wanted to watch it that evening. 'Wanted' was a bit of a strong word, Satine thought, as she switched on the television set and waited for the image to spring to life. The sound came on first and she recognised the annoying Breakfast show D.J. from Radio One who was presenting this week's Top of the Pops. The grey image of the cramped studio came to life in a few moments and Satine vowed then and there that she would buy her mother a colour television for her birthday. After all, the income from her current role was the best regular wage she had ever managed to secure, and her contract had just been extended for a whole year.

 She looked at the eager faces of the youngsters that had been placed around the little stages of the BBC set and noticed two young teenagers who were standing right by the annoying D.J. They two young girls had clearly battled their way to get right by the presenter, knowing that they would be on camera and broadcast to the nation. They waved and blew kisses, clearly revelling in the fact that it would make them instant stars at school the next day. The cameras moved away from the girls, their few seconds of fame fleeting but so wonderful in their eyes. The next chart hit was played, a video of a live recording by an American band who were clearly unable or unwilling to lip-synch their way through their latest in the BBC studio. A chart run down from number twenty to number ten followed and then the screen was again filled by the irritating D.J. who had now acquired a feathered headdress to remind the audience of his 'zany comic genius.' As expected, the two teenagers had been elbowed out of shot by another couple of camera-hungry youngsters who were now waving and laughing their way to their own playground glory the next morning. Satine leaned forwards as the D.J. spoke:

'And now, live in the studio is the highest climber of the week! Leaping 27 places to number six – it's Mixed Emotions!'

And there, dressed in the same costumes as she remembered were Mixed Emotions miming to 'Mixed Emotions.' The dance routines were exactly the same, with Claude prancing around to the delight of the hordes of young girls. The BBC had clearly insisted on a little waistcoat, but he was bare-chested beneath it. Cicely stood proudly centre-stage, her beaded costume glittering under the studio lights. The rest of the stage was filled by two female singers, one black and one white. Satine could not be sure if they were wearing the exact same costumes that she and Ava had worn, but she would not be surprised if Rosie had chosen the women to fit the existing costumes. Their voices were very low down in the mix compared to Cicely's, but it was clear that the song had been re-recorded, and Ava and Satine's vocals expunged. Whether the replaced harmonies were actually by the two new group members was anyone's guess. S.K. may well have drafted in a cleaner from the club who could carry a tune to lay down the tracks.

The song and the routine came to an end and the camera pulled away and back to the D.J. who mused: 'Mm! Hot stuff there from Germany! They've already burnt up the charts in France and Spain. Will they be number one next week?'

Satine turned off the television and closed her eyes. She pondered on how she felt about the whole thing now. Her emotions were definitely…. mixed. Above all, she could see Ava in her mind, beautiful and full of joy and hope as they set out on their adventure to Hanover. She mourned Ava every day and knew that she would for the rest of her life.

She opened her eyes to see her husband standing before her, wet tea-towel still in his hand. Although very busy and successful in his own right as a sound engineer at Abbey Road studios, Iodine clearly did not deem his work to warrant an escape from pot drying duties.

'Are you okay? I said it was probably not a good idea to watch it.' Lukas sat down next to Satine and kissed her tenderly on the cheek.

'No, I'm glad I did. Claude looks well; Cicely too.'

'We could still meet up with them before they fly out. They said they would be at their hotel all night.' Lukas already knew what Satine's answer would be to that suggestion.

'No. I'll call Claude later, maybe.' She rested her head on Lukas's shoulder, knowing that she probably wouldn't make the call when it came to it. Lukas kissed the top of her head and they both sank back into the sofa.

 Satine closed her eyes again, seeing the image of the two eager teenagers waving into the camera in the Top of the Pops studio, their ecstatic faces shining with the certainty that this was the best moment of their lives so far and who knew which of their wildest dreams could come true under the spotlights?

Who knew?

www.ingramcontent.com/pod-product-compliance
Lightning Source LLC
Chambersburg PA
CBHW051508120626
46551CB00012B/827